CHANGING AGE,
CHANGING MINDS

Valerie Leung

Valerie Laws (http://www.valerielaws.co.uk) is a poet, playwright, novelist, performer, and specialist in sci-art installations and commissions. She featured in BBC2's *Why Poetry Matters* and performs worldwide live and in the media.

As well as IAH, she is also Writer in Residence at Gordon Museum of Pathology, London, funded by Wellcome Trust. In her Arts Council-funded *Quantum Sheep* she infamously spray-painted poetry onto live sheep. She is the author of ten books.

Changing Age, Changing Minds

Valerie Laws

Writer in Residence

for the *Changing Age* Initiative

at the Institute for Ageing and Health

University of Newcastle upon Tyne

First published in the UK in 2011 by

Institute for Ageing and Health (IAH)
Newcastle University
Campus for Ageing and Vitality
Newcastle upon Tyne
NE4 5PL
United Kingdom
http://www.ncl.ac.uk/iah/

Cover image: composite photo of
Elsie Richardson MA and Jack O'Hagan
Cover and text design by Andrew Edwards

ISBN: 978-0-9555755-2-5

Printed in the UK by Martins the Printers

CONTENTS

PREFACE

By Professor Tom Kirkwood

New Ways of Looking at Age

Ageing is extraordinarily familiar yet much of what we thought we knew about ageing is changing. The continuing increase in life expectancy has exploded the confident predictions of demographic forecasters, made as recently as the 1980s, that human life expectancy would soon hit a ceiling. Science is revealing that human ageing is much more malleable than we used to think. And we are – still too slowly – starting to recognise that increasing longevity is indeed one of humanity's greatest success stories and not some ticking time bomb of incipient demographic catastrophe.

It is very fitting therefore that Valerie Laws' wonderful book, written in connection with Newcastle University's Changing Age initiative, should mark another important milestone along the path to looking openly and honestly at what ageing means in today's world. Valerie Laws has been a brilliant Writer in Residence at the Institute for Ageing and Health. The hallmark of Valerie's work is its freshness combined with a readiness to look closely at all that the science and experience of ageing entail. Growing older is not always a bed of roses. It brings increasing vulnerability to some very unwelcome disorders, many of which Valerie has made both more real and perhaps a little less frightening by looking at them squarely, without evasion or denial. Throughout, Valerie's work is grounded in an essential humanity that celebrates the joy of being alive at any age.

The Institute for Ageing and Health is proud to publish *Changing Age, Changing Minds*.

Professor Tom Kirkwood

Director, Institute for Ageing and Health

THE INCREDIBLE SHRINKING BRAIN
(For my mother, Sheila, who taught me living and dying)

Excited, she tugs me up to her bedroom of thirty years.
'Look! There's all this here!' A sweep of her arm presents
Melamine wardrobes with fancy handles, the swagged
Pink curtains she sewed herself. Back downstairs,
'Look!' The hall: plates painted at an evening class
She took to keep her brain alert, ranged on the delft rack.
'See? It's all gone! But look!' Upstairs again,
A miracle – her bedroom's reappeared, like
An MFI-bought Brigadoon. The universe in her skull
Is shrinking, big crunching; and true to the predictions
Of physicists, her time is running backwards, rewinding
What she knows and understands. Something she learned
Playing peep-bo with her twin in the scullery kitchen
Is about to vanish, but she holds it for a moment,
Poised between knowing and not knowing.

She's amazed, her bedroom might still exist when
Out of sight; soon, she will unlearn this too. But today,
As her time runs backwards to a singularity, it feels to her
Like discovery, and today, I try to share her joy.

Valerie Laws
Published in *All That Lives* (Red Squirrel Press 2011)
Exhibited in IAH *Coming of Age* (IAH 2011), as part of
Slicing the Brain, an installation poetry sequence.

AUTHOR'S INTRODUCTION

I became Writer in Residence at Newcastle University's Institute for Ageing and Health (IAH), as part of a personal journey investigating firstly, the science of death, dementia and pathology, and later, the brain, how it functions and ages. My journey began with experiencing my parents' deaths: my mother's from Alzheimer's, during which illness I helped my father care for her, then his sudden death from an unsuspected aneurysm less than a year later. After Residencies at Gordon Museum of Pathology in London, at Kings College London and in Leeds hospitals, it continues through my current Residency at IAH. Their ground-breaking *Changing Age* initiative is at the heart of my Residency. The original outcome for me was to be poetry on the science of dying, which resulted in my audio visual installation *Slicing the Brain* at the associated *Coming of Age* exhibition, performances at the IAH and related venues, and my full poetry collection *All That Lives* (Red Squirrel Press, 2011). *Changing Age, Changing Minds* grew naturally and organically out of my Residency too, of which more later.

I have come to know a lot more about the science and the experience of dying, but also about living, and how closely they are connected, something modern society prefers to forget: ageing and dying seem to represent 'failure' for technology and medical expertise, so often concerned with 'conquering' disease. Ageism is rife in an ageing population, a sad irony, and one notably tackled by *Changing Age* and its Charter. I also came to know the indomitable spirit of many older people I met and worked with, their powers of endurance, courage, and commitment. Over and over again, after a matter of fact description of a life peppered with tragic loss, poverty, cruelty, and struggle, I have been told, without irony, a variation of 'I've been so lucky. I've had a wonderful life.' This serene perspective alone sets this generation apart from our young, with their genuine despair about having the wrong kind of phone, and the 'devastated' contestants who fail to win *Pop Idol*. All the more harrowing then, the recent reports of old people left starving in our hospitals by indifference and poor organisation.

As rapidly developing technology changes society at an increasing rate, there is a corresponding tendency to assume that any individual's life experience is obsolete before we can learn from it, and hence older people and their acquired knowledge are in a sense left behind by the rest of us (as if we are not them, further down the line!). This is questionable – my own forebears' dread of debt and devotion to self-respect, despite grinding poverty, was temporarily forgotten by succeeding generations, with appalling results. The attitude to commitment of older couples to each other and to their children is also striking – in some ways a bad thing, leading to years of abusive relationships with no escape, but in other ways, a lesson to us all, as cheerful self-sacrifices abound to care for loved ones right to the end.

But there is so much more to older people's contribution to society than the wisdom experience has given them, what they have done for us in the past, their endurance through war and want. They are still contributing now, in their millions, to the tune of billions of pounds each year, to society, in the fields of paid work, voluntary work, caring, childcare, and more. (See Elsie Richardson's piece in Chapter Two for more on this.)

My experience made me keen to support *Changing Age* and its accompanying Charter, so when I mentioned writing a book, and Dr Lynne Corner suggested it might be intergenerational, *Changing Age, Changing Minds*, was born. It was not until I began to research and collect material that I realised how much it is needed. I led some writing workshops on ageing with Year Seven and Year Ten school students. I expected a mixture of responses, working with students who were enthusiastic and delightful. I was not prepared for my first experience of this subject. They were asked, as a warm-up in a writing workshop, to simply write randomly on big sheets of paper, words that come to mind when they think about ageing and older people. When we shared the results, I was frankly staggered. Virtually every word was negative, often perjorative, laced with distaste for an appearance, a condition we all, with luck, will experience. Disability was strongly associated with age, although it happens to all ages: two prejudices reinforcing each other. Use of 'cheap' services like buses, or pound shops, was further evidence of old = 'loser'. Laziness, stupidity, and worst of all, exploiting the young, were other accusations. Here is a brief extract from the list:

'Death, coffin, uncontrollable bowels, saggy, walking stick, pensioner, oap, nursing home, countryside, grey, wizard, cripple, tea, wrinkly.'

I was careful to show no disapproval, but I did remark on the general negativity and particularly on 'relying on the young', as the young I was standing in front of were (naturally) yet to make any contribution, but seemed unaware that the old, after a lifetime of work in most cases, were still contributing to their support, rather than the other way round. So, where does this negativity come from? When the students went on to write poems or short pieces about the older people, usually grandparents, in their own lives, the result was very different. A generation of jeans-wearing, curry-cooking, motorbike-mending, pocket money dispensing, joke-making, treat-devising, much loved and respected older people appeared. I found this kind of result with different groups, in the two age ranges I worked with. In one straw poll, with one group of fifteen students, I found that of the significant older people in their lives, thirteen looked after them in loco parentis: ten used computers to go online: fourteen still drove: and seventeen worked, nine paid, eight unpaid (one did both!).

There seems to be a mismatch between younger people's personal experience of ageing in their own families, and their general attitudes to ageing. What's the source of this mismatch? Is it the media, the barrage of advertisements treating ageing and wrinkles as a disease to be hidden and eradicated? Supposedly funny portrayals of old people as clueless abound. Shreddies breakfast cereals are 'knitted by nanas'. This campaign began merely as patronising, showing stereotypical white-haired old ladies happily knitting Shreddies in some vast sweat shop factory. Subsequent ads have shown them as stupid as well as gullible, needing a man to tell them what to do, and being too dim to understand the corniest of jokes. We have been invited to mock their attempts to look attractive. This is just one example. Perhaps adults are attempting to be 'down wiv da kidz' by inviting them to join in with mocking the generation above. But even governments, constantly feeding the media with stories about the 'burden' or 'problem' of an ageing population, is doing its part in promoting the idea of useless old bodies cluttering up our society. They would do well to remember that the old have votes... These stereotypes are fast becoming obsolete themselves in the real world: multiple marriages mean that some children have fathers in their sixties, while men and women are getting together with partners widely different in age, both younger and older. Children from infancy upwards are still being presented with pictures of 'grannies' and 'grandads' who are very old indeed, whereas their own grandparents may be in their forties.

The young people I was working with are helpful, kind and well intentioned on the whole, and many schools encourage their students to get involved with older people, often by visiting care homes and entertaining the residents for example. Praiseworthy as this may be, it does tend to strengthen the stereotype of older people as purely recipients of charity and care. So I make no apology for using most of this book to introduce the reader to a range of older people, many of whom are fabulous stereotype busters, to remind us all of what real achievers older people can be. As well as respecting their experience, wisdom, endurance and past contribution through hard times, and respecting the need some of them have for care due to failing health or dementia, let us also remember that many, including those just mentioned, are still contributing, working, creating, studying, gaining qualifications, doing research, caring for grandchildren so their children can work, caring for spouses so the state doesn't have to, imputing values and extra attention to the young, skyping, emailing, living independent lives, still dating, still having sex, and still having fun.

As I researched this book and met more and more fascinating older people, I chose to devote the bulk of the book to their stories rather than those of the youngsters, feeling that today, younger people's voices are heard more than those of their elders. Interspersed with young people's pieces on ageing, the older people's stories that follow are often funny, often moving, fascinating glimpses of a world gone by, but also of how the old embrace the modern world and enrich it by doing so.

The scientists who have been so generous in sharing their research findings and expertise with me, I hope will also enjoy this book, and perhaps it will in some small way flesh out their professional interactions with older people, or their post-mortem brains, to show more of the whole persons involved.

E.M.Forster said, 'Only connect'. We can pretend, in order to discriminate, that those with disabilities or who look different are somehow 'other', 'not us', which is bad enough, but it is ludicrous even to attempt this with ageing. We will be them, moisturise as we may. We are all ageing, all the time, from birth onwards. We should not apologise for living longer, but celebrate!

A NOTE ON MY METHOD IN WRITING THIS BOOK.

I interviewed older people either at home, in the case of some individuals, (some of them participants in the IAH '85+ project', a cohort now 89/90), or in day centres run by charities: Age Concern (AC), Alzheimer's Society (AlSoc), and Dementia Care Partnership (DCP). I have indicated by these initials where contacts were made, at the beginning of each individual's piece. From my notes, I wrote their life stories, some as interviews, but most of them in the first person, as if in their 'voice'. Their names and some details have been changed to protect confidentiality, except for those few who are in the public eye in some way or who chose to use their own names. The young people wrote their own pieces, mentored and edited by me.

I have made the decision to group the contributors' stories into loose categories, though many of them could have equally been placed in several or even all categories. I've done this with a view to 'stereotype busting', a primary motivation for this book. Speaking of which, though not technically 'old', I was disabled at 32 by an accident. This has given me awareness of health problems, attitudes and threats to independence usually associated with ageing. In my research, I have met many people over 80, and even over 90, who walk better and further than I can.

A NOTE ON DEMENTIA.

I have placed contributions by participants with dementia in the same way as the others, apart from a few advanced cases dealt with in the 'Vulnerability' chapter. My decision to indicate where or through which organisation an interview took place, has the added function in the case of 'DCP' or 'AlSoc', of identifying which participants have some form of dementia. I consider this a good thing, not to enable readers to make allowances, but rather to show how much those contributors can still recall, share and teach. Two things have most commonly been said to me by lay persons about dementia over the years I've been studying the science of dying. One of them is, 'you can't die of it'. This is untrue, as I know from my mother's death certificate. The other is, 'well if I get that, at least I won't know anything'. This is also untrue, as readers will see. The truth may be less comforting, but it is vital to face these facts if we are to give proper treatment and respect to those of us who develop dementia.

STYLE AND GRAMMAR.

To keep the pieces flowing like listening to conversation at a bus stop, I've chosen not to set them out with separate paragraphs for dialogue, and have only used quotation marks for speech where the context makes it unclear when the person being quoted has stopped speaking! I have chosen also not to write everything in dialect, though the dialect will come through in the language, rhythm and structure, but where dialect words are markedly different to standard English, I've written them phonetically (eg, 'iz', the Tyneside term for 'me').

CHAPTER ONE

YOUNG MINDS, AGEING WORDS -
HOW THE YOUNG FEEL ABOUT AGEING AND OLDER PEOPLE

Here is the complete list of words about ageing, referred to in my Introduction, produced spontaneously by school students. They were sitting in groups of four, five or six, so I put a large sheet of paper on each group's table, and in as neutral a way as I could, simply asked them, as a warm-up exercise, to write randomly any words or phrases that came to mind when they thought about ageing or older people. Nobody knew who had written what. The results were not what I would have expected.

Here we go!

'Wrinkly, mobility scooter, Oap, Senior, day centres, smoking pipe, elder, knitting, wrinkly, werther's originals, false teeth, pension, old people's homes, very breakable, dependent on the young, very forgetful, walking sticks, grey hair, decrepid, shrivelled, frail, ancient, ill-mannered, life support, balding, sewing, sagging, dependent on drugs, wrinkles.

Death, coffin, uncontrollable bowels, saggy, walking stick, ramblers, pensioner, oap, nursing home, countryside, grey, wizard, cripple, tea, wrinkly.

Old, oap, saggy flesh, bingo wings, wrinkles, slow, zimmer frame, frail, white hair, old hearing aid, will, Elvis, dementia, care home, caring, walking stick, incapable, stop growing hair, nurse, wet the bed, glen miller, ww1/2, cowboy films, frank Sinatra, whisky, cute!, dominoes, sweets, tissues, plastic hat, glasses, housebound.

Decrepid, out-casts, ww2, stupid, care home, when I was your age, blinding, un-able, bananas, during the war, reminiscent, critical, wheelchair, bingo, tartan, chairlift, shrivelled, oap, shopping trolley, cats, raffle, hypocritical, elderly, tea, daytime tv, gold card, alzheimers, hobnobs, public transport, naptime, balding, rapping grannies, coffee morning, afternoon tea, countdown, nostalgia, zimmer frame, stereotypical, Vera Lynn, care home, slow, lifeless, dribble, granny, walking stick, knitted stuff, out-in-the-old.

Wheelchair, wrinklies, 44 bus, specs, walking sticks, nivea anti-wrinkle, antiques, hospitals, bananas, toffee, rocking chairs, songs of praise, old, glasses, frail, jumpers, mature, wise, grey, Elvis, bowls, mugs of tea, bingo wings, zimmer frames, peppermints, bingo, biscuits, microwave meals, white hair, pension, bungalow, dentures, meals on wheels, slippers, 86 bus, mobility scooter, knitting, grandparents.'

A barrage of stereotypes and negative images, only 'mature' and 'wise' being clearly positive. Asked what 'old' meant in number terms, one or two said over 80, most said 60. And one, late fifties! Yet one boy's father was in his sixties, let alone grandparents.

Surprising not only the ageism, but that the stereotypes are so old fashioned. It seemed odd for this generation's grandparents. Also many words are about disability which could apply to any age – I had a 'walking stick' and so did a boy with an injury! Interestingly, they thought of older people as helpless and dependent on the young, though I pointed out that most of their grandparents are working or doing charity work or childcare, paying taxes etc, while they, the young are actually depending on them!

After some discussion, they wrote about an older person they know, and what kind of old person they'd like to be. Writing about their grandparents or older relatives, a very different, much more positive, much less stereotypical picture emerged. I speculate in the Introduction about why there should be this mismatch between how the young feel about 'ageing and older people' and, for example, 'my nana' or 'my gramps'. See Chapter Four for a selection of tributes to the significant elders in their lives.

CHAPTER TWO

EARNERS AND LEARNERS – OLD AGE ACHIEVERS

OLDER PEOPLE STILL WORKING, DISCOVERING NEW SKILLS OR
KNOWLEDGE, OR GAINING NEW QUALIFICATIONS.

ELSIE RICHARDSON, 84

PHD student, activist for older peoples' rights,
University lecturer, Psychotherapist, all since her 70th year.

I'm doing a full time PhD course, I do some University lecturing, but I'm a
passionate campaigner for older people's issues and rights, prominent in many
organisations. I'm 84 and going blind, but computer technology helps me keep
going with my studies and activism.

I've been Chair of North East Older Persons Advisory Group (OPAG) for
two years, a member for eleven years. OPAG arose from a government initiative
and now we've become a cooperative, it's older people acting for older people
which is unusual, it's usually old people being acted *for*, but we have a voice
and we can speak for ourselves! We report to Change Agents UK Ltd, our
umbrella group. We meet regularly. I'm Chair of England OPAG as well so when
all the regions' chairs meet, I'm Chair of the Chairs!

I'm also Chair of Years Ahead, for eighteen months now. It began eight or
nine years ago as the North East Forum on Ageing, up to five years ago when it
was renamed. It used to be about older people's issues such as poverty, but we
now focus on demographic change issues which involve older people. We have
task groups to focus on different issues, such as transport, isolation – isolation
has stumped every task group I've known, it's hard to know who is affected and
how to reach them.

And I'm Vice Chair of NPC Northern Region. National Pensioners Convention is a nationwide organisation with three million members. Every May, we have a pensioners' parliament in Blackpool, three thousand members come from all over, we invite ministers and MPs and question them. They usually come, though occasionally they don't! They take it in their stride, they get shouted at and called names, but politicians can always answer. We bring forward resolutions, some go into early day motions, and if we are lucky, to parliament and become Bills, so we do have influence. NPC get funding like any charity. We used to have a direct link to the Deputy Prime Minister's office, there was always an 'older person's champion', we have had Alistair Darling. It's a waiting game to get them to deal with all the issues. We now have a National Older Persons Advisory Group, (nothing to do with OPAG), every forum in the regions of England has a representative on there, they meet and report on what they achieve. So we still have a voice to speak to government. It's run by the Department of Work and Pensions, so it's a government organisation.

I'm also on the board of NDA, New Dynamics on Ageing. It's led by Sheffield University and consists of older people *doing* research - not *being* researched, but doing it. We involve ourselves in projects with the university. We've been doing some research on nutrition in hospitals, for example, and our findings go to the British Society of Gerontology.

All these meetings keep me very busy. Looking at the last two weeks, I spent two days in Derby for OPAG, two days in London for NDA, another two days in London for NDA. I've also been to Government offices in Gallowgate, for two meetings. I've also had two meetings at Northumbria University for my PhD, I'm in my final year of the three year course, working on my thesis. All these meetings also involve writing reports afterwards and so on.

I also give lectures to other groups about the conferences and other projects. I also wrote a paper with two others, 'Do we eat or do we heat?' That paper is now in the British Museum and the Bodlian at Oxford University. That will happen with all my projects and papers.

More about my PhD studies, I have to write eighty thousand words this year! I work at nights, sometimes until 2am. My thesis is on 'Influence of older people in policy making in 21st century'. You see, many boards nowadays have 50%

older people on them. For about two years now, this has been the in thing. Of course older people are delighted to be sought after. However, sometimes they are tokenistic, they know nothing about what's really going on and are just expected to rubber stamp decisions taken beforehand behind closed doors. Those people feel they are being used. I'm interviewing boards all over the UK; so far, in Scotland, London, North East, and I've still got to do Wales and other areas. So far, two are pleased with respect, equality and ideas acted on, but one is horrendous. They hear what has been done but have no say. I also interview the other policy makers.

This takes every spare minute. I have deadlines. I have two supervisors, in the Gerontology Dept at Northumbria University. And I meet them once a fortnight. I have it all typed up ready for my meetings to go over word by word.

I'm going blind and registered partially sighted so this is hard work. I need special computer equipment to help me, an electronic magnifier and new 'my read' to read papers and books. As an older person's activist, I speak out to government ministers. I go asking for funding and they know I'm an activist. Years Ahead are funded mainly by Newcastle University and also DWP. The NPC will get funding from anywhere. It's getting harder with the cuts.

I've been to Number 10 Downing Street to meet the Prime Minister at a cocktail party. A group of us were invited to lunch at Richmond House, and the minister for pensions was there, so I had a jolly good go at him! Then fifteen of us were invited to Number 10 for cocktails. All of us were activists on behalf of the elderly. (I used to be on the executive of the National Insurance Workers Union for five years before I retired, the first time that is!).

This was two years ago. I spoke to Alistair Darling, the chancellor. There were lots of ministers there. The PM, Gordon Brown, shook hands with everybody. I couldn't see his face, I can't see yours now, but when he got to me I got close enough to see him and he looked awful! I didn't mean to say it but it just came out, I said 'Prime Minister, you look as if you need a big fat hug!' And he gave me one! I nearly fell down. His wife was very charming. A lot of disabled people were there and she knelt on the floor to talk to them. As they walked around, what made him seem more human, he walked with his arm round her waist. But I'm a trained psychotherapist, and I feel he has a nasty side. It was my instinct. That he wasn't a nice person.

I didn't get my degree until I was 73! When I was 75, I got my Masters degree, but I didn't enjoy it. You see, I did my BSc(Hons) degree at Northumbria, and spent the three years laughing! I had a great time with the other students! They included me in everything they did. I've been to some funny places! I loved it. I graduated with my BSc in Human Organisations when I was 73. But when I went on to do my Masters, I had parties here at my home for the fifteen students, they still email me. But there were only two of us who went on to do the full course, the others stopped at the diploma stage. So it wasn't as social, not as much fun as all the BSc brainstorming sessions and socialising. My Masters degree was in 'Post Natal Depression' and it qualified me as a psychotherapist. I vowed I'd done my lot getting that far. Then three years ago, I was lecturing to young doctors and health students, and my supervisor on the collaborative gerontology team got her doctorate, and I went to her congregation ceremony, and she mentioned that there were two bursaries for PhD students and persuaded me to go for it. I was so angry about older people being used tokenistically, I thought, if I get one, what a shot in the arm for older people, they think older people are brain dead! So now I'm nearing the end of my PhD and will be 'Dr' Elsie Richardson when I'm 85, with luck. It's a tremendous lot of work.

As for paid work, well I've been lecturing at the university for the past 6 years, a paid position as visiting lecturer. I lecture to the new intake every year. Also I do research with the University Fellows, at Northumbria. We work with researchers in South Africa, Germany, Australia, we have video conferences. Our findings are being published in an international nursing journal. I'm also collaborating on several books, through the Joseph Rowntree Trust.

I'm qualified to do paid work as a psychotherapist. I don't take on many patients, I have one at the moment I'm giving therapy. I did my Masters degree in Guidance Counselling. I also have to do six lectures unpaid as part of my PhD studies.

I'm also on the board of the University's Education, Health, Community and Service Users, or CHESS. We have meetings for that too, and I'm invited to all the graduation ceremonies etc. I've been lecturing on older people's issues, challenging the assumptions of the students about ageing. Sometimes they are hilarious. They are very bright but unaware. We have experience of living to offer.

Six or seven years ago, we did a 'house for life'. We got a council house for six months to make it suitable for an older person with full adaptations. It cost £40,000 to do. We had all the state of the art equipment. People came from all over the world to look. We showed what could be done with modern technology.

My greatest asset is living for 84 years! Older people are regarded as a burden. But older people save the UK £86 billion per year! In free services, childcare, caring, voluntary work. That's an NPC statistic. Ken Livingstone, who was Mayor of London, told me that statistic years ago, it was less then, it's been going up steadily. Gordon Brown borrowed £86 billion from the pension fund, from all of our NI contributions, an interest free loan, I've never heard that he's paid it back.

Computers, I've used them since I was 70. Now I'm on my fifth! When I started the BSc I had no idea. I went to learn, on top of my degree studies. Now I use it for research, the internet, emailing, writing reports, finding statistics.

Now I have serious incurable health problems, especially my eyesight. I'm going blind. The computer and the adaptations to it are making it possible for me to carry on my work. I have special equipment for reading and magnifying so I can read books on my pc screen. I have macular degeneration in my eyes and am registered partially sighted. I also have diabetes, which has been quite a problem, making me ill. I have spondylosis at the top of my spine, and degenerative arthritis in my knee and hip joints so I can't walk much and use a stick. I have a hearing aid in each ear, I only use them outside the house. But it doesn't stop me travelling up and down to London and elsewhere, going to all those meetings, writing reports and lobbying for older people! I get taxis, and use special assistance on the trains. I live independently in my own bungalow. I manage most things myself, cooking and so on. I have a device to put on my cup so I know when it's full. My three daughters are very helpful and kind. One of them who lives nearby cleans for me and cuts my lawn. My daughters are wonderful. One of them keeps a holiday free for me every year, last time we went to the Caribbean. I love the heat!

The secret is, do what you always did, and don't think any different. My granny used to say, don't keep going to the doctor, your body will put itself right. Of course as you get older it gets less able to do that. But they're researching it now.

So since I was 70, I've done a whole university education to lecturer level, gained a new work qualification, become part of so many organisations and become an activist. It's like I started a whole new life at that age, as if I was starting again.

Before that, I worked as an Administrator for the Prudential Insurance Company for 21 years. I spent nine years at home bringing up my daughters. I had my youngest at 40! I was married for 33 years. My husband suddenly died when still in his fifties. My youngest daughter was only 16, she found him, lying on the landing. He had a tiny scratch on his hand, some bacteria got in, it was a 10 million to 1 chance, it took four days to destroy him. By the time they found out what it was, it was too late. I was 22 when I got married. I always

Elsie graduates.

would have liked to go to university, but the war was on. We loved our lives during the war, a lot of people did. But it stopped me going to university, though I matriculated with 10 passes and could have gone. Then I married.

So I have a great deal of work to do, paid and unpaid, my studies to work on, travelling for my work and for holidays. I go to the theatre a lot. And I keep on speaking up for older people and our rights!

NORMAN CORNISH,

World renowned artist and 'pitman painter', still painting at 91.

'My pictures go for £30,000, the big ones, £10,000 the small ones.'

I've been a professional painter for fifty years. I'm 91. Before that, I worked at the colliery, but selling paintings as well some of the time. I worked 32 years at the colliery, down the pit. I worried about giving it up, I had a wife and two kids, and we lived in a colliery house, we were saving up for our own. Whenever one of my pictures sold, I put the money in the bank. Slowly it accrued and over 12 years we got enough to get a house. The mines were closing anyway, men got shifted from one to another, I think the colliery bosses hoped some got lost on the move! The last one I worked in was very wet and very very unpleasant. I did a week there, my pains got worse – I had pain in my arms, legs, back, years of hewing coal underground, I had a spinal jacket on – I could hardly get out of bed, but had to do full shifts. Every shift was an Olympic effort. I wasn't working easy, 'on the button', but working at the coal face. You competed with your marras, to hew more than them! The colliery was running down. Sarah was very encouraging and supportive and said, 'get your notice put in! you'll be a cripple if you don't, and if you don't put your notice in, I will!' So I went to the local for a couple of pints Dutch courage and I got the bus down. Well they wanted shot of us! We were already looking around at houses, our two kids had seven years between them, so my daughter was 16 and my son was 9, when I left the mine, after those 32 years.

When I started down the mine, I was just 14. The Spennymoor Settlement had just got started, and I heard about it, 1931-2 it was. A shop down this street had a poster up advertising a show of work by the Spennymoor Settlement Sketching Club. I went to see and join up. They were all older men. Bert Dees, a good watercolourist, said come back when you're fifteen! So I went back next year. He was smoking his pipe, he was going to say no again, when the warden, Mr Farrell, came and saw 'this little black-haired boy full of enthusiasm' and that's what he wanted, young people with enthusiasm. They also did languages, crafts, skills, drama down there. So at 15 I joined the Sketching Club and carried on working down the pit. The media called my exhibition, 'The Pitman's

Academy', and I've always been considered 'the pitman painter'. For years I made as much selling paintings, or more, than down the pit! But I kept that name long after I went professional. They assume you'd be too thick to do anything creative, people like me. Sid Chaplin the writer was another one. They don't say 'Strauss – the banking musician!' I said that on TV. They assume when you become an artist you'll be a primitive artist. I've an international reputation, honorary degrees. An MA from Newcastle University, 1974, and a Doctorate (with Tony Blair!) from Northumbria in 1995, and I've an MBE.

How did I learn my art? I was mostly self taught. I've never been to art school, except as a lecturer. I just drew continuously, and learned from the Settlement. Recently I was invited to see the play 'Pitman Painters' as a guest. It gave the impression they were all rough and ready men, the writer got cheap laughs at their expense. But those men asked for Robert Lyon to come and teach them, so they'd know about art when they went to see art galleries! These were clearly intelligent men. I sat there in the middle and watched 'Oliver Kilbourn' with a lady telling him to leave the pit, she offered him money, but he 'couldn't leave his old world'. In fact I'd done exactly that, with nobody offering me money.

I remember old Mr Miller in the pit, he worked on a button. Sometimes in-bye, there'd be a bit time for a bit chat while waiting for machinery to be moved, and he talked to us about Roentgen and the invention of X rays. Another man had qualifications to be a Colliery Manager, but he stayed on the button. Also Benny Copley invited me round with my banjo, and I didn't play it, he played his piano and he was brilliant! And of course Sid Chaplin was a very good writer. Wherever you are, people are the same. If two thousand men work down a pit, they are the same as everyone else – some clever, some not so clever.

I was born just after the First World War, in the Depression. We had a good life, climbing on slagheaps and trees. Our parents shielded us from the Depression. I'm the oldest of seven kids, I passed to go to Secondary School. My Dad was out of work, we struggled to survive, so they couldn't afford for me to go to college. In secondary school, you stayed on until 16, instead of 14, people I knew went on to be doctors, solicitors. I had to leave at 14, and start to earn, I wanted to earn to help my family. My father got a job at the colliery and got me set on there. So I started down the pit. When I signed up, this fella said to me, 'you've just signed your death warrant, son!' My first day down the pit, I started on Boxing Day, at 3am! The pits were open every day then. To get there I had to walk two miles in pitch dark by meself, I was terrified. I was glad when it snowed, it lightened it all up so I could see. When I got there it was terribly noisy, men shouting numbers for their lamps (safety lamps, but hand lamps, not helmet ones then).Then I had to get a disc, well they were like soldiers' dog tags, they were to identify you if you got killed in an accident down the pit. I looked up and above the door was a big framed poster by Robert John Heslop, of a cat, and 'a cat has nine lives, you only have one – take care of it!' You can imagine what that felt like, seeing that. Then I went through the door, and saw the men with their lamps, climbing steel steps onto a steel gantry, they looked like fireflies trapped in a steel web, this first vision of the pit hit me hard. (Later I painted that scene and it became a successful painting.) Then I went to the pithead and I went down in the cage with the men. It was a dicey pit, a lot of accidents, and injuries. And one time I remember hearing someone shout, '82 men killed at Easington!' But you got used to it. I used to draw down the pit, the side of the tubs, and on the concrete shaft bottom. I used chalk, or some soft rock, like sandstone on steel tubs. I'd ask me marras to draw three random lines, and I'd make them into something. People'd see them about, they'd say, 'there's one of Norman's!'

So I was mainly self taught. But Bill Farrell, the Warden at the Settlement, he'd been an actor, Mrs Farrell was a teacher, he was good at lots of things, and he'd say strange things to me which made me think. We had Durham County Library in the Settlement, with a row of art books, and that's where I learned about art, Van Gogh, Monet, etc. Bill Farrell said 'draw what you know!' He was a socialist. I picked up a magazine which had a mural in it, by Frank Brangwyn, a sailing ship unloading. I said this is marvellous. Bill said, 'no, you are a better artist than him!' I thought he was mad! He said, 'Brangwyn's a better designer than you, you are a better artist.' He said I should show people the world I know. Bert's brother Jack Dees showed us a complex painting of the Lakes. I said to Bill, this one's marvellous, and he said, 'do you know, I'd rather have one of your little drawings than a hundred of them.' So I learned from him and the books. Also we had no money spare, so when we had exhibitions at the Settlement, we'd frame them cheap in old frames that people didn't want. I painted a scene, a view of red roofs, an open gate against green, I saw it more as a pattern than a picture, it looked a bit like a poor Matisse. It was exhibited and a lady who lived in a Hall nearby, she said, that's great, but it should be in oils. Bill said, we can't afford oils. She wrote a cheque for ten guineas to buy oils and brushes, I shared it with the others of course. So I painted my sister, my first oil painting, at home. It was crowded, there were nine of us living in effectively one room, a two up, one down. It was hard to find space. Me mother was making bread, she was always baking, washing, it was hard for her, I showed her my painting. She wiped her brow and looked. 'Oh, it's alright.' Anyway the group went gaga over it, they were whispering and I could hear them saying, 'if he can do this now…' and that encouraged me. The Laing Art Gallery in Newcastle held an annual exhibition, it was like the Royal Academy of the north. It was called 'works by artists of northern counties'. The selection committee chose them. Famous artists were invited to exhibit, such as Lowry. My little painting was hung in that exhibition, between two big paintings by professionals, their colours were bzzzz! My painting looked like a little black flag hung there!

Then war came (1939). We were kept down the pits and not allowed to enlist. The government was determined to keep the arts alive, not allow all the horror to destroy them, so they organised lunchtime concerts, and exhibitions and so on. The Settlement had famous pictures on loan, and we had a little theatre there, the Everyman, and we exhibited there. Stanley Spencer, Augustus John. I used to help to hang them – so I learned a lot about how to hang an exhibition, it's not easy you know. Few years later I was invited to London, for an exhibition called 'Art by the Miner'. I was asked to look after it. Attlee was Prime Minister, they'd just nationalised the mines. I got to know Dr Evans, who bought five of my paintings for the NCB (National Coal Board) offices in London. He asked me, what do miners do? I told him, and he decided to hold this exhibition, from all over the country. It was to be in Oxford Street, the Academy Cinema, they had a big room in the basement, it had to be all cleaned out and painted, we couldn't hang anything as they kept painting the walls! We couldn't get them hung, anyway, in the end I had to do it, so that experience in Spennymoor was useful.

I was invited to go on TV, 'Picture Page' it was called. At that time there was only television in the London area! This was sixty years ago. It was on afternoon and night, filmed at Alexandra Palace, 'Ally Pally'. I met Richmal Crompton, who wrote the 'Just William' books, she was there with the William actor. There was a radio programme, called 'In Town Tonight', and they just moved the format to TV. Richmal Crompton had a walking stick. So we went to a restaurant and I was amazed to see nobody helped her with her tray and so on. So I did and we sat together and talked. She was very nice. This was 1947. So Dr Evans's assistant took me back to a big house in St Johns Wood, there was a lovely woman with long black hair, her husband was a painter who became an RA. I was given a cup of coffee, I was scared of spilling it and they were all chattering and name dropping famous people, Graham Sutherland etc. I was fascinated they knew them but fed up of balancing the cup so I put it down in the fireplace, and soon they were agog to hear about coal mining! I used to draw the drama group at the Settlement too, plays from all over the world, Sean O'Casey, Ibsen, I learned a lot from them, about other nationalities. All this went to teach me to be an artist. And of course I drew continuously.

I went into local pubs and they were always busy then, and I'd draw, they got used to me and ignored me. Wonderful subjects just being themselves. They made wonderful shapes with their gestures. People would say to me, why not go to the South of France? I didn't want to! I liked the people round here. Melvin Bragg made his first programme round here, in his 20's. He was filming shots of the pit for the arts programme 'Monitor'. Becoming known, for me, was a slow process. I got better known, through the exhibitions, the TV and so on. There was only BBC1 and then in 1959 suddenly there was Tyne Tees TV. Soon I was invited to go on an arts programme and I got friendly with the producer, we called him 'Lew', he was Kurt Lewenhak. A picture I did of my daughter was on the programme. She was 10 then. I was interviewed by Valerie Pitts. They put Vaseline on the glass of the painting to get rid of the reflections. Then the Stone Gallery opened in Newcastle, and they asked me to exhibit. For the next twenty two years, I worked at the colliery, and the Stone Gallery sold my paintings. Sometimes I got more for art than coal! This one time, I was doing overtime down the pit, ten, eleven hour shifts, it was 'stonework', putting in girders to hold the coal face up. This Friday, we got our pay and there was something missing! Oh it was a dicey pit. There was half a crown missing out of the £12 for the week's work. I got home at 6am, absolutely knackered, when I realised the pay was short. I had to double back and go straight back to the pit to argue so they didn't do it again. While I was getting ready, exhausted, been working all night, to go all the way back, a letter arrived from Stone Gallery, with a big cheque in. It was equivalent to six months wages down the pit, but I still had to go back and argue about the half crown, to support me marras!

So when I made the decision to leave the pits, Black and Decker had just opened a factory and some of my family went to work there, I thought I could always get a job there! Jennie Lee had just been made Minister of the Arts. I saw the Arts Officer for Durham, and he got me a job at Sunderland Art College. Just one day a week lecturing in life drawing. He said, 'it's four ten', I thought well four pounds ten isn't much but Sarah said, go and do it. So I did, for the experience. When my first pay cheque came, it was fourteen pounds, not four ten! And it went up to sixteen. I got more for that one day a week lecturing than a week working down the pit. I did that for three years, as a visiting lecturer, while painting and selling paintings. It was hard sometimes, and it's terrifying not knowing if money will come in. I fell out with Stone Gallery, they took up with Lowry, anyway I could tell you the tale, but I stopped using it. But people would come to the house and buy paintings. Sarah did all the money stuff. She'd tell people a price, I always thought it was too much. An American couple came, she said £40, they said we'll have two then! So when I got an honorary degree, I was invited to a Congregation of the University, and I met Councillor Theresa Science Russell. She asked me, 'why no exhibitions Norman?' I was nearly 70 by then! I said I'd fallen out with Stone Gallery. She said, 'we'll have to have one at Northumbria University (then Newcastle Polytechnic), for your 70th birthday.' She invited Mara-Helen Wood, of Newcastle Gallery, and Tom Bromley and others to the Civic Centre for lunch to set it up. I worked very hard to do enough paintings for it! It was very successful. I said to Mara, (it wasn't then a selling gallery, it was an educational gallery), 'could you be my agent and sell my work?' Soon we had to register for VAT! She's still my agent twenty years on.

I still paint and work on compositions. I have a bit of a balance problem, it's the cerebellum part of the brain, it's just age. I had another big exhibition for when I was ninety, last year! Pam Royle did a piece on it for North East Tonight on TV. We donate paintings to galleries for the public to look at, quite a few to Northumbria. Mara's also director of Kings Place in London and I also exhibit and sell from there. Well, my pictures go for £30,000, the big ones, £10,000 the small ones. Reproductions of them go for £400.

So I've been very successful, but we stayed in this house, (a terraced house in Spennymoor), we've been 43 years here. Upstairs there's a big study, used to be a vicar's, with a north light, which is my studio.

Sarah and I have been married for 63 years. We still live independently. Our son and daughter and their partners see us often.

AUTHOR'S NOTE: Norman showed me his studio, very tidy. He's working on a big picture of a group of men in a bar, he showed me sketches, and how he maps out the picture with a grid. He explained about composition, and what draws the eye to details. The mens' pints of beer glow like amber lanterns. His fingers are long and strong looking. The forefingers are curved inwards a bit, but otherwise, despite decades of hewing coal in the wet, they are remarkably undamaged by arthritis.

World renowned artist Norman
Cornish, 91, and his wife Sarah.

Norman Cornish b1919
Self-Portrait, Charcoal, chalk on paper
53.4 x 44.8cm, Private Collection
© Northumbria University Gallery
on behalf of Norman Cornish

ELAINE PERRY

Despite her comparative youth, (66), Professor Perry is included here partly because, as she retires from a world renowned career as a pioneer scientist and researcher, she is still in the early stages of major new projects outside the lab. But also because, her and her husband's combined careers, partly at IAH, led to the development of drugs still used to help people with dementia. They also raised a family who have shown scientific, medical and artistic talents.

Elaine and her husband Robert were flamboyant figures in the 70s and always have been, and are still stylish and dramatic people, anything but the stereotypical 'man in a white coat'. Elaine had to combat sexism as she climbed the academic ladder, as liberation and equality took some time to penetrate the defences of the ivory towers of academic biomedical science!

Elaine is a Professor of Neurochemical Pathology at Newcastle University, in other words she studies brain chemistry and how those chemicals enable our brain cells to pass information (such as memories) one to another along neural pathways. She has just become Emeritus Professor after a very distinguished working life, as she retires from University lab work after forty years. However, she has her own sphere for further pioneering discovery, in the form of Dilston Mill Physic Garden, and this will go on using and expanding Elaine's knowledge of the brain. This unique project (now a Registered Charity) is a collection of over 800 living, growing plants, in a beautiful part of Northumberland. These plants all feature in folklore of various world cultures, as having special properties to aid our health, brain, and mood. Physic gardens of herbal remedies have a long history and are still around today. The difference is that Elaine researches the folklore of each plant and finds out 'the science bit' – if, and how, the plant chemicals interact with brain chemistry, to produce real effects which can help us keep our brains alert, keep our mood relaxed and stress-free, and aid healthy ageing. This blend of hard science and folklore potentially acts as something of a 'rare breeds farm' of well-known plants, as newly discovered plants of power are rapidly copyrighted by major drugs corporations, putting them out of the reach of most people. The garden can be visited and is used for courses in herbal knowledge, creative writing, art etc. Despite ongoing problems with her vision which she combats with computer technology, Elaine has many plans for her 'retirement' centred on this aspect of her work.

These include controlled testing of herbal teas for anxiety alleviating effects; exploring herbs that maintain animal health; involvement in new monastic garden in Hexham abbey; incorporating new subjects and inspiring individuals in her annual courses programme; enlisting artists to add new dimensions to the garden such as glass mosaics, a giant sundial seat, a stone arbour for enjoying aromatic plants, and a guardian garden angel.

Elaine's working life as a Professor, after gaining a PhD from Cambridge, has involved working with a team including her husband Robert Perry, originally a cardiologist, who is an equally distinguished Professor, though of Neuropathology, which means he dissects brains and studies changes within, including those caused by various forms of dementia. Elaine and Robert were at the forefront of a small team based in Newcastle, who did early vital work on dementia, showing the link between behaviour, and physical changes in the brain, and implicating the lack of a normal brain chemical vital for memory (acetylcholine). Most importantly, this led to finding a way of replacing it, at least for a while. This led to the development of drugs such as Aricept, still a standard drug today, which can halt the progress of Alzheimer's Disease and

Elaine and Robert as young star scientists.

Elaine, with the author, in her physic garden.

prolong the useful and enjoyable life of dementia subjects for significant periods. This work began some years ago but has branched out in various ways, eg new brain imaging studies identified a marker to differentiate Alzheimer's Disease from Dementia with Lewy Bodies in patients. Robert has done ground breaking work in identifying different forms of dementia. Elaine's specially created part time post at King's College London led to new lab work on stem cells - the ability of the brain to generate new stem cells even into old age. This has provided new hope that drugs may help the brain repair itself in this way. Elaine has also been working on the nature of consciousness. She has won many prizes and has lectured world-wide. Elaine has written and edited many books and scientific articles which have been widely published throughout her career.

Her future publications are intended to be less academic and more accessible to the public. She herself is working on a range of books: *Botanic Brain Boosters, Young People's Guide to Health and Happiness with Herbs* and *Herbal Health for Animals*

FRED, 73

Professional and home cook, still working as a chef for Age Concern,
while caring for his wife.

I'm 73. I work as the cook here, Mondays and Tuesdays, and Wednesdays at another Centre. I cook a two course hot lunch for the Age Concern day centre clients. I work about 10.30-1.30.

Before, I was working at Durham University, Collingwood College, as Chef Manager, we provided three meals a day to 300-400 students every day. I retired after I had a stroke, I was about 63. I was healthy up to then. So I relaxed for about two years, until my wife retired as a cashier, by which time I was 65. My wife's not keen on travel so we worked in the garden and around the home. Anyway, after a while, I felt I needed to do something more, and I saw this part-time job advertised, 'cook wanted', as a jobshare. I enjoy this job, I've done it about 7 years now. I always say, you have to enjoy a job to do it well. Especially this one – in catering, your work is other people's play. I was my wife's carer after she had a stroke, she's better now but I'm still her carer. These days she manages by herself the few hours I'm out of the house though the stroke has affected her memory and she gets panicky when I'm not there sometimes. I feel better to be earning a bit of extra money, and getting out of the house for part of the week. Being a carer is stressful. We both helped care for my wife's mother when she had Alzheimer's Disease. So I still work, but this job's easy after cooking for hundreds!

I've always been interested in cooking - I did all the cooking in our house when I was married, unusual for a man in those days! I've taught my three sons to cook as well. When I was at school, we had separate schools for boys and girls. Girls did cookery, boys did woodwork! But times were just starting to change, and in our last year, we were offered a choice, girls could do woodwork and boys could do cookery, but we had to go to the girls' school to do it. About twelve of us signed up, I think mainly to be with the girls! But at home, my mother would get us boys helping with the meals, making apple pies and so on. She was a cook actually, she worked in the first Chinese restaurant in Newcastle! The food wasn't totally Chinese, more Anglo-Chinese, perhaps because it was the first. It was down by the old city wall near China town, then they moved to Gosforth. So as she worked, she needed us to help with cooking and cleaning, sweeping etc. But if I'd not been offered the chance at school, I'd probably not have done it for a job. When I left school, I heard there was an apprenticeship going at the Turks Head in Newcastle. They did businessmens' lunches there, more than dinners. I can do cordon bleu cookery but I prefer to cook good plain food. So I worked there and did my apprenticeship. Then I had to do my national service, so I joined the RAF and became a cook. I cooked for the Air Commodore and his wife, he was in charge of Andover Camp, an officers' training school. I cooked for them and their guests, officers' dinner parties. I got married while I was doing National Service. After that, I worked at Proctor and Gamble, catering for their staff. And in the evenings, I worked for a couple in their home. They advertised, they were surprised when a bloke turned up! I was like a housekeeper, cooking their evening meals for them, I did that for 12 years as well as my day job, before I started my job at Durham University. At Durham, we had to cater for different cultures and religions and diets. We had international dinners prepared by students sometimes, each made a dish from their own culture. Cooks will say, 'I don't like that!' I say you have to know what something's supposed to taste like, even if you don't like it.

So when I'm not doing this job I'm my wife's carer and I work in my garden. My three boys are all grown up and I have grandchildren.

JACK O'HAGAN

Child star, then a world famous dance band singer, now at 90 a keen user of the internet and computer gamer: *'I have over a hundred computer games!'*

I was a singer with dance bands, I performed all over the world, I made records. I started as a professional singer at the age of ten! I went on tour, earning good money, as the head boy in a singing group called 'Twenty Eton Boys', we performed in Tom Moss' Revue. The Revue owner contacted my mother, and it was agreed I'd go to school in whichever city or town we happened to be in! Then I was in a group called 'Steffani's Silver Songsters', we played music halls and concerts with Ronnie Ronald, a famous whistler.

How did the Revue know about me? Well I was one of eleven children. My mother and father were very good singers, not professional though, and my aunts, uncles, cousins, and all of us, we all sang and danced. Our house in Felling was right by the church, we could see it from the window. Every Sunday, after Benediction, my parents and dozens of people all came back to our house to hear us and join in the singing, my uncle played piano. The place was heaving! And we did concerts for charity. My mother had aspirations towards show business, she took me all over to competitions and so on. My brothers Gerard and Vin also became professional singers, and my cousin, they were in the same troupe, but after me. So that's how I went on tour with the troupes. People said I was too young! Although I was earning good money, it all went for my sister. She was terminally ill, she was ill for four or five years, and there was no NHS then, it cost my parents a lot of money for medicine and doctors. She died when she was 21. She was seven years older than me, and then after me were six more. I've been slim all my life, but when I was born, I weighed 14lbs 2oz, my mother was charging admission for folks to see me!

Well we weren't poor, we didn't want for much, we were fed and clothed, but we had nothing much else. For our holidays, we'd go to Whitley Bay every year – for one day! But we didn't miss anything because we had each other and we had love for each other. But with all those children, my father worked all the hours God sent, he was a workaholic! He was a wood turner, very skilled, very clever at designing things. He made one of those wooden dogs on wheels with 'walking' legs and moving ears long before they were on sale. And he'd make beautiful standard lamps. There wasn't a problem he couldn't solve. I had a very clever grandfather, he made me a bogie, the envy of all the boys, it had a steering wheel and brakes. My father worked for his firm in Hebburn until he was over 70, and he played war when they finished him. I still have a brother and sister alive over the river.

My mother lost three babies at birth but we didn't know about them until years later. My mother would disappear for 2-3 days, and suddenly there was another baby in the family! And we adopted a brother as well. My grandmother, my mother's mother, who lived with us all with my grandfather, she would deliver babies, like a midwife though she had no qualifications of course. One day a mother died in childbirth. Before she died she asked my gran to look after her child. So my gran brought Billy home and he became an O'Hagan. There were no adoption papers then! Billy would go to the Town Moor Fair if he was short of money, to the boxing booths, they'd challenge people to fight and win money, he'd come home black and blue but with his money!

My education? Well even though I was touring and in different schools all the time, I was top of the class, I was good at lessons, but my education finished when I was 13. It's never bothered me. I was good at algebra, but I've never used it! Yes, I had my singing to make a living from. So I was in Steffani's from about 13 to 16 when my voice broke. When a boy's voice breaks, he has to rest it for two years. I was lucky, my voice came back! When my voice broke, I went into my father's firm and served my time as an apprentice jig and tool maker, a good job in engineering. It should have taken five years, but after three, war broke out and I volunteered for the Navy. I was in a reserved occupation so I didn't have to go, but I wanted adventure. I was on an aircraft carrier. My rank was EA4 , just below Chief Electrical Artificer. Harland and Wolf built the vessel, in Belfast, and we were stationed there for two years while they built it. Then we went into action. We covered the invasion of Salerno. We had to go through narrow straits. We were dive bombed by a German pilot. He dropped bombs just either side of us, and our 22,000 ton ship rocked right over ! We were all battened down below. We also went to Trincomalee, now Ceylon I think. We became a repair ship for aircraft later on.

But during the war, I was in great demand as a singer! I sang everywhere we went, and I sang in the American servicemen's canteens. I sang in one in Sydney, Australia, and I was offered a contract by the editor of the Chicago Times, to go to the US after the war. He'd give me six months' work and publicity, then it would be up to me. I had several offers to go to America. There was a famous all-girl band, Ivy Benson's Band, he asked her to ask me to go but I still said no. I had a wife and family at home by then! I earned a lot of money singing, so I was very popular, the other men would borrow money from me! After the war, I sang with Roy Fox and his band. I'd sung before with Peter Fielding, at the Oxford Galleries in Newcastle, I sang with him after and then toured with Roy Fox. Later I worked with Max Wall, a very famous man in music hall, in his revue, 'Over the Wall'. Then with Oscar Raybin, the Blue Rockets, I was singing with the world's biggest dance bands. I had my fifteen minutes of fame! I sang in a nightclub in London called the Millroy, where I sang regularly for Princess Marina, the Duchess of York. She'd come in with Noel Coward, Ivor Novello, Stewart Grainger, lots of big stars. She'd send a bottle of whisky to my table. She'd ask me to sing her favourite, 'Night and Day,' I'd sing it for her maybe half a dozen times! Yes, I was away from home, a lot of the time. I didn't see much of my wife and children. You had to be strong willed.
(NOTE: Jack's photos show a very dapper, handsome man!)

I was forever being admired. There were lots of pretty girls. They'd say, here's my keys, Jack! But I always said no. Sometimes we'd play at Newcastle, or near enough to commute, and we got a holiday on Good Friday. This went on for years, until my voice started to give me trouble, and my wife Betty had four children to look after. She told me she wanted me home.

I met Betty when I was singing with my brother in Wallsend, he said he knew a great little dance hall at Denton Burn, and we went there and that's where I met Betty and asked her to dance. We married in 1942 and we were married for 57 years. I miss her terribly. She died 12 years ago. That's Betty.
(NOTE: he points out a sepia photograph enlarged and printed on canvas, stretched on a box frame, on the wall. A very pretty woman, in a veiled 40's hat, looks over her shoulder at us, smiling.)

Betty was in the WAFS in Scotland during the war. We married there, in Dumfries. Our eldest son was born 7 years after we married. We were apart during the war. Then I was touring with the bands. We had three boys and a girl. They've all done well. My eldest son lives in Las Vegas, he's floor manager of a big casino. My second son is a financial advisor with a major bank. My third son sang and toured with the QE2. His wife was chief buyer for Next and Principles. My daughter is a manager for a big cosmetics company in a big department store. Some of my grandchildren went to university.

So anyway, I was pretty healthy, but my voice started to go and now I can only whisper, they call me Whispering Jack. I smoked, for years, until my granddaughter, when she was ten, said, 'you're going to die, Grandpa!' So I stopped. Years ago now. I'm not much of a drinker. My father was in the trenches up to his knees in water in World War 1, he'd give his rum ration to the cook for extra food. I'm the same. Though I like a little tipple of whisky now and then. And we had rum in the navy.

So after I gave up singing, I trained as a capstan operator at Vickers, on constant nightshift. I didn't like it. I had a good knowledge of music so I learned to play the organ, and ended up teaching it full time. There was an organist called George Charlton, he was called 'the Reginald Dixon of the north east'. He had a music shop with six to eight organs in one room which people could take lessons on. I learned to play with him, then I started teaching, I'd walk around plugging in earphones to each one to hear the pupil. He had dozens of pupils. George went bankrupt though, so I taught at home. I played the organ and had one at home until recent years. Then I became a rep for a TV company which refurbished TVs and radios, and I'd sell them. Then I worked for Benders Optical, aluminising telescope lenses. Betty and I had a house in Kenton Lane, then we moved here to this flat about 22 years ago as it was too big for us. Eventually Betty became ill, she was ill for four years. I looked after her for two years. Then she ended up in a care home for 18 months. It became my home. I never missed a day, I was there with her all day, every day, until she died. After she died, my son said, 'we don't want to lose you too, you need a break,' and he invited me to Vegas for six months. I played golf there, the courses are out of this world, I played golf until last year when I was 88.

So I live alone and independently. My daughter visits and my family visit and keep in touch, Age Concern send someone to spend time with me and I go on their outings. I've been very healthy, though I've recently had two stents put in my arteries in my chest, but they say my heart is perfect. I've macular degeneration in one eye and the other is having injections. I had a brain scan and lumbar puncture after I woke up just a little while ago with a terrible headache, they didn't find anything.

Anyway, my second son and the others were saying, you've got to keep your brain active. So they set me up with this – a 37inch TV screen linked to a computer, a keyboard with big letters on the keys. I'd never even considered it! So they got me all the equipment. But I learned how to use the computer and the internet. I just picked it up! My family was like that. I found out how to use the internet, and order things from it. I got this series of books, *PC Knowledge for Seniors*, and I worked through them. Now I've got over 100 computer games, that's how I spend most of my time! I like 'shoot em up' games. My friends say, when are you going to grow up?! *Wolfenstein, Assassins Creed 2, Just Cause, Jericho*… and games like solitaire. I've got *Big Fish* games, great for training your observation skills, it's a hidden expedition, you have to solve puzzles at each level, very complicated fantasy landscapes, with hidden clues to solve. I send emails. I use skype to talk to family. I have had all my old music recordings transferred onto my computer, so I can play them.

(NOTE: Jack plays me a recording of himself singing and playing the organ.)

Here's one of me singing when I was 18! This is Betty's special song. She loved this one.

(NOTE: Jack plays a recording of himself singing *Good night, wherever you are*, and he waves to Betty's picture.)

The pianist on that was Billy Hutchison, Tyne Tees TV musical director. You can still buy my records online! My younger brother Vin O'Hagan sang with the Ken Tones, they sang on the Six Five Special on TV. He sang at a Royal Command Performance.

(NOTE: Jack plays me an example of this, again from his pc files, and also his son singing on the QE2, with a swing style band.)

I played golf until last year, now I play snooker twice a week. I do exercises every day. Me and Betty liked to mix with young people and learn new things. I've had a good life. My only regret is losing Betty. It's God's will how long I'll live. Long life is in my genes. My father, 99. Mother, 95. Grandparents both sides, 90s. My brothers and sisters lived a long time except for my sister who died at 21 and another who died in an accident in her sixties. I pray every night for my family. I can still touch my toes and I do a whole lot of physical jerks every day. My granddaughter Lyndsey just won th*e Look & Lorraine Curvy Supermodel* national competition, I'm still walking about three foot off the ground!

(NOTE: he demonstrated some tap dancing type exercises, still very supple and active. Jack was featured in the *Evening Chronicle's Nostalgia* magazine, Issue 6, as *Man of song – Jack O'Hagan.*)

Jack today with the young Jack, singing star.

Keen computer gamer Jack ready to play.

CHAPTER THREE
CARING AND SHARING

Older people, both men and women, save the state a fortune by caring, often full time and with little or no state support, for family members with disabilities, often to the detriment of their own health. Here are a few examples.

TED AND LAURA

Ted, 81, is full time carer for his wife Laura, a wheelchair user who cannot walk or speak after a stroke twelve years ago. (AC Day Centre)

I talked to Ted, who is carer for his wife Laura, who was also at the day centre but chose not to be at our interview. She cannot speak, just makes sounds, though is fully compos mentis. Ted is small and wiry, sunburnt, ruddy faced, thin, with startling blue eyes, platinum rather than grey hair, energetic and mobile. His long commitment to care for his wife, with all the frustrations and sheer physical effort, is nothing short of heroic.

TED'S STORY: I'm Laura's carer. She uses a wheelchair, she's paralysed down the right hand side, and can't speak, since a stroke twelve years ago, since when I've looked after her. A careworker comes in each morning to bath or wash her but they often turn up late or are new and don't know her. One day a week, a Thursday, we have a sitter service, a sitter comes for three hours in the afternoon so I can get out and have a bit time to myself. I generally go for a walk with an old mate of mine from work. We used to go along the river, but now I'm getting pain in my legs if I walk more than a little way. I have to go out to the shops and so on as well, other times I can leave her for very short periods. She looks at telly, she looks at magazines but she can't read text, she can get up and hold onto the furniture to get herself to the toilet. But she can't wipe herself. I have to do all that sort of thing for her. I have to cut up her food. The hardest thing is, she can't talk. All that comes out when she speaks is 'ba ba ba', it sounds like speaking and she means something by it but that's what comes out, whatever she wants to say. Sometimes I can understand her, like if there's something to go on, if she can point to something for example. She can use her left hand. But she can't write, most of the time random letters go down on the paper. We have a scrabble board and she tries to make words, the sitter does that with her as well. Mentally Laura's quite good, but that means the frustration is worse. She used to be a very pleasant woman but now she has no patience and gets annoyed, it's so frustrating for her to be unable to communicate and to depend on being looked after. She used to go to a 'speech after stroke' club, it was good, they'd take her each way, and I'd get most of a day to myself but she fell out with them, over a jigsaw, and wouldn't go back.

The wheelchair is hard work for me, yes, especially as I'm eight and a half stone and she's nineteen and a half! You can't get it up kerbs and so on. It's hard to push it. She had one they'd widened for her for about five years, then they insisted on her having a stronger one, said she's too heavy, just covering themselves, but that means the wheelchair is that much heavier itself, so it's harder than ever to push it. She was only 55 when she had the stroke! She's 67 now. I'm thirteen years older than her, I'm 81 now. You'd have thought it would have been me. But she had high blood pressure. Then one day, I'd just been into town early with her mother to get her bus pass renewed, we used to look after her mother, I was back home by 10.15, I made a cup of tea, Laura was busy in the bathroom, I called, 'your tea's ready' - no response. I went in and she was stuck, on the floor, couldn't speak. The ambulance came, they had a job getting her out of the bathroom which was small. That was August 18th and she came out of hospital on 23rd December. I said to them, how am I to manage, they said 'if you don't she'll have to go in a home', I couldn't have that. So I got on with it. You've got to live day to day, try not to worry. But I'm going into hospital to see if they can do anything about my legs, I worry what'll happen to her if I need to stay in, or if anything happens to me. I mean, she can't speak, so how can she let them know what she wants? How would she explain about needing the toilet? She won't wait, she's very impatient. The carers come, often they change them, she gets annoyed if they can't understand, she gets fed up and just loses her temper, but can only go 'ba ba ba'. She gets up each night to go to the toilet, at least once. I never get a full night's sleep, I have to get up with her. For six months she's slept on one of those reclining chairs, it's been better than the bed. She shouts for me when she needs me. I might miss her in the bed when it turns cold! We've been married 41 years. I'd retired when she had the stroke. She had the high blood pressure for some years. She had tablets for it. When I think back, I never heard that the doctor told her anything about what might happen, that she should take more exercise. But in fact she'd just started Weightwatchers and had lost a few pounds. She never liked exercise, I always loved walking but she'd take a bus. We had a great time for six years after I retired, we used to go on bus tours to Scotland or Torquay or Newquay.

We had three children, but we lost a laddie when he was 17. It was only 8 months after that, she had the stroke, so it might have been a factor. It was one New Year's Eve, we'd been out with another couple to a party, we got home and then two police came to the door, to say he was dead in the hospital, a drug overdose they said. We've a son nearby, he comes every Sunday with his two kiddies, sometimes Thursdays. He's a househusband, his wife works. And we've a daughter further south, she comes up in a campervan on the way to the countryside, visits for mebbe three hours each way. When I was young, everybody round here lived near their relations. Til Mrs Thatcher said get on your bikes and find work.

I used to take Laura out in the country, in the wheelchair, we'd go along the river at Newburn to Wylam, or Prudhoe, there are good paths there, except when there's a bit of a ramp or a curve it's hard to keep it steady. And now it's more difficult with my legs. And I have a bad back problem. We go out for drives though. She can get in the car and I put the chair in the boot.

I was 40 when I got married, well, three days short of my 40th birthday. Yes it was late to get married, I was always a shy sort of person and had lots of friends but never seemed to meet lasses much. My mates'd get married and I'd make new ones, go to the working men's club. Anyway, Laura and I went to the same Church, and she lived in the next block down my street. This Christmas Eve, she asked me to take her down to Midnight Mass, escort her you know. Yes, so she'd feel safe out that late. Yes, she might've been making a move! So we went together. Next week she wasn't there, doing overtime at Vickers Armstrong, clerical work. Week after, I asked her to the pictures. It was a cowboy film with Sean Connery in it. At the Haymarket, Newcastle. We were courting about 18 months before we got married.

Well things are difficult but what can you do? It's hard when you're dependent on careworkers, and hard for Laura and me. We get on quite well. I'm not complaining.

IRENE, 85

After a long life of youth work and a strong Christian faith, many years of caring for a much loved disabled husband and working partner, Irene is comfortable with death and the dying. (AC Day Centre)

I'm nearly 86. I've osteoarthritis and I'm hard of hearing, so you'll have to speak up! I live in a two bedroomed flat. I'll have been widowed 19 years come October, I was married for 43 years. I miss him. He was a church Pastor. We worked together in Shieldfield, South Shields, all over. I wouldn't live in South Shields though, we went over every day. We had a big youth club there, over a hundred members, there was one for 8-14 years old, and one for 15-21. And I looked after Denton Burn 'Over 60s', took them on holidays and all sorts. Oh, well I was 56 when I started that, and I did it for ten years. So I was older than some of the older people! I thought it should be someone even older running it actually. I nursed my husband for twelve years, pushed him in a wheelchair for nine years, after he took a stroke. I'd taken courses, First Aid, St Johns Ambulance, all sorts, for my youth work. The doctor said, 'You've saved this government a fortune!' Well in the end my husband had two weeks in the hospital, they sent him home but then I had to get him back in. They kept us waiting in A&E, then we got into Ward 2, we'd only been there twenty minutes when he died, of his 14th stroke. He was 65. Oh, yes, I was with him. But I knew, you see. I used to empty his bag into the pail every morning, and that day, there was no water, his water was all jelly, so I just knew then. The district nurse came in, and his blood was all jelly as well. She left, and I ran down the passage and called her back. I've been with so many dying people, it doesn't bother me. I visited one woman, she said, will you put your hands over mine, and say the Lord's Prayer? So I did. Someone who was there, said, oh, she'll not die yet, but I called her nephew, and he and his wife came. She just said, 'I'm finished', lay back and died. Am I religious? No, I'm a Christian. The difference? A religious person goes to church, but a Christian accepts Christ as their personal saviour, as I did at 17. Oh, no, I'm not afraid to die. I'm quite ready to go when the Lord takes me. We had no children. My husband had a cancer tumour in his prostate. I decided I'd rather have him, so they took it out! We looked after everybody else instead. I looked after my niece's two children, while she worked.

Well me and my husband started in Prudhoe Street Mission. He got £10 a week, and I got £5. I did the visiting from Crawcrook to Bedlington Station, including the hospitals. I used to run netball as well. The sports master would ring up, to get me to bring a team. We'd play matches against the Catholic church team. My husband was orphaned at 2 years old. His grandmother brought his sister up but she put him in a home, he was in Ponteland Cottage Homes until he was 16. I couldn't like her after that. Well she couldn't really take them both, she had no room, but she should've kept them together. How it happened, both his parents drowned, at Tynemouth. His dad was in the navy. That day, they left the children with the grandmother, and went to the beach, and never came back. His mother dived in, and his father dived in after her, and neither came out. They'll be buried there, there'd be no identification on them. There was a baby as well, who died in the General Hospital, after they died.
(NOTE: I couldn't help wondering if this double drowning was a story told to the boy to explain his parents' disappearance which may have been from some other cause.)

But my family made him welcome into our family. When he met my husband, my brother said to him, 'it's Friday, we're taking you to the football tomorrow!' And they kept doing it for years, all the brothers and brothers in law. Mam always said, 'there's no such thing as an 'in law' in this family!' My mother was 49 and a half when I was born. One of eleven children! Mam and Dad were both Sunday School Teachers. I'm 4ft11inches tall! And my sister was only up to my shoulder. Have I been deaf long? Since I was fifteen, when I got ear ache, Mam put warm oil in my ear. My mam delivered babies and laid out the dead.

Regrets? Well you sit and think... I'd like to have had children. But it wasn't to be. I had my husband. What do I like to do, well I used to walk and walk, for miles and miles! I like TV, you can learn a lot from TV, I love quizzes, oh yes I love University Challenge! But TV can do a lot of harm as well. And we do activities in here. I love to read, I'm reading a book by Gladys Aylward, who brought all the children out of China. She gave the book to my brother! And we talk in here, I get on well with Eileen and the others, oh I'm mouthy, me! But I think the world's all upside down now. I want to say to people, you're missing the joys of life, the coast, the countryside, the birds, God's creation! You should be out enjoying that instead of boozing in pubs! Oh, I've never been a drinker. Recently, I've had a lot of bereavements, but somehow me and the family, we've all clung together. My nephews visit, and phone every week.
I feel I've had a full-filled life!

EDITH, 79

A lifetime of caring for her mother, now her elderly brother cares for her.
(DCP Centre)

My dad worked down the pit. I'd to polish his pit boots when he came in. He'd come home all black, we'd get the tin bath out in front of the fire. I had two brothers, three sisters, one of them has dementia and is in a care home. I never married. I worked at the brewery for so long, didn't like it, then at the Guardian Royal Exchange Insurance for 25 years. I loved that, they used to have dances every so often. I stayed at home and looked after my mam, until she died when she was 87. She was in a wheelchair for two years after breaking her hip, then she couldn't eat, and went into hospital. They found she had cancer in her throat. They give her four months to live.

I'm nearly 80 now, and I'm in this wheelchair! Four months ago I was rushed to hospital and went into a coma, not getting enough oxygen, I've got a ventilator at home now. My chest is bad. And I'm nearly blind. My brother, 70, looks after me. He never married. He takes me out in the car, and sometimes me, my brother and cousin all go to stay for a week at Kielder Forest. I love that! I'd love to be able to see, but I'm happy! I used to read magazines, now I get Talking Books. I come here twice a week, my niece works here, she told me about it.

DAVID AND JOAN

Live independently in the country with their animals. David, musician and Solicitor, cares for his wife Joan, an artist, historian and writer, who has Alzheimer's.

David and Joan are clearly both very intelligent and highly educated. They have been married 47 years. They have a horse, two goats, and a dog. David was a solicitor, and is a keen pianist. Joan brought up the children but also worked at the University giving continuing education classes. She also published books and her MPhil thesis on local history, specialising in the history of child labour. Joan is a keen artist, who still paints. Someone from Dementia Care Partnership comes regularly to enable Joan to keep painting. Her paintings hang framed all over the house, and unfinished ones are propped up here and there. They show a clear change in her style as dementia has progressed over the last four years. The earlier works are more representational, accomplished pastoral scenes, soft, misty outlines, autumnal colours. The latest are in layers like strata, nests of concentric shapes, in very bright, hot colours, very primitive abstracted landscapes, and those with buildings show a change in perspective, with an 'opened out' effect almost like cubism. Oddly enough these layers in bright colours look like the layers in the brain slides I have seen at my Residency. David said that Joan usually paints from photos, but nowadays often leaves the photo behind and goes off on her own tack. This is truly fascinating and a rare chance to see what dementia does to perception.

David had told me that Joan is sensitive about dementia and prefers 'not to have it' so I promised not to confront her with it. He was able to tell her the truth about my visit, as I'm interviewing older people in all kinds of states of health and fitness. We were able to discuss the topic of dementia, and Joan was comfortable with that, she kept talking about her mother (who died a few years ago, a typical dementia sign in itself), saying that 'she has dementia' and I got the feeling Joan might be signalling she's aware on some level that she has it. Joan became very emotional about David and how much she loves him, again, I felt she was aware how dependent she is on him and how hard it is for him. Very like my mother, Joan is very articulate and friendly and warm, but very restless. She is unable to sit still, constantly getting up and putting her coat on to go out, 'to the University for a meeting', and needs distracting or diverting. David shows some signs of stress and tension in his body language which I recognise from personal experience, sometimes forgetting words and names, all due to exhaustion and inability to relax due to the relentless demands of the illness. They were both very welcoming and kind to me.

I started the actual interview by asking about their attitude to getting older.

JOAN: you have to hang on in there the best you can, try to keep going, do things that relate to the present, and not to the past. I keep active. Yes, my art is important to me. We both have to look after our mothers now.
(*Both mothers died years ago.*)
It's a lesson in how people need to keep their brains ticking over. There's a slight worry about losing your mind, like my mother did towards the end
(*her mother died at 94*). You just have this gut feeling... you just do what you can.

DAVID: you are quite driven, darling.

JOAN: yes I suppose I am. I love David very much, he's a number one person. I feel very well! We've got animals, Molly the dog...

ME: and Bob the horse! (*who is 37 years old*).

JOAN: Bob the Bugger! He likes to drop his shoulder and throw people off. He's done that to quite a few people!

DAVID: we had another horse, a welsh cob, Rachel. She got epilepsy and had to be put down.

JOAN: I teach courses at the University, continuing education.

(David says she used to, not now.)

JOAN: thank goodness I've got a supportive husband!

David goes to fetch a huge book. It's Joan's MPhil thesis, ('An Inquiry into the Lives of Children in Rural Northumberland, 1800-1914.') It's dated 2004, six years ago. David said though Joan's had dementia for four years, it was diagnosed as depression for a long time by a GP and treated as such for two years, and he had to fight for a diagnosis. Strikes me it might be because she's so high functioning in her speech, which might easily mask AD.

DAVID: I stopped work in 1998. I wanted to play golf properly, and do more of my music.

JOAN: that slightly put me off!

DAVID: so she went back to do research. She was already in the field of child migrants. She published a book, a pictorial history, in 1995. She wrote two published books before she did her thesis.

JOAN: it was a relief when I finished them! You're never quite satisfied with what you do, are you? He's been very good, though, David, an absolute brick, supported me all the way.

David fetched another book, 'Newcastle upon Tyne, a pictorial history', to show me. Dedicated, 'to my husband and family. 1995'.

DAVID: Joan got a letter from the publisher, out of the blue. Phillimore. She was tutoring for the Open University in local history at the time. She also wrote 'Our Bairns', about child migrants. Joan went to Canada in the early 90s to follow up child migrants from Stannington Farm Colony School, where boys were trained and then sent to Canada til the 1920s, Australia til the 1960s. They were very ill treated, some Christian Brothers ran a camp, Fairbridge Society were involved... Joan found some boys were never heard of again, or badly abused. She was sent an unpublished book by a woman child migrant telling her story. Also Joan transcribed 'Diaries of Wm Brewis of Mitford', which were published by Wagtail Press.

David couldn't find any copies of 'Our Bairns' but he brought a copy of this book. Joan began reading out snatches of it.

I asked David about his music and what time he had to pursue it.

DAVID: oh, classical music. I've a Bechstein Grand piano in the house. And an electronic piano I can take when we go away. Well we do get away sometimes, maybe a cottage type holiday. And our son, a jazz musician, was recently ordained, and we went to see that. And I have a group of musician friends, we meet up to play music, well that's lapsed now for me. And I play for a singer, she's just done her Masters. We did a concert at the Lit and Phil, and we're going to do another. She's a good singer and, er, well adjusted to the situation. (*meaning Joan's illness*). Music gives you a focus, and goals. I did voluntary work for some years after retiring, a school, 3 or 4 charities, using my legal expertise. Until it got out of date. Just before I was 70, I had to give it up. You have to be aware when that time comes (*legal knowledge out of date*) or you are no help to anybody. An ideal day, well it would include painting, music, our animals – but *now* everything takes three times as long. There's a great inclination not to accept the illness, and to feel things could be restored, but one becomes unreasonable to the other person. It took a long time to dawn on me that one has to accept it's progressive and not going to restore. I heard all the words people used about it, but learned very slowly what that means. I try to be more tolerant and understanding. If I get cross, at least she forgets! And she forgets if she gets annoyed and calls me every name under the sun!

JOAN: yes, David really is a number one person, I love him so much... I just hope we can stay together until the end.

Joan becomes rather tearful, David gently says 'now then, darling'. I ask Joan if she's become more emotional, with age.

DAVID: Joan was reticent and understated, though I always knew how she felt... but lately she's become more emotionally open.

JOAN: David has great qualities of truth, and seeing clearly who needs help. He does everything he can. He sees peoples' needs.

ME: did you always live in the country?

DAVID: we lived in Newcastle before moving here. Joan had the horse....our youngest son the jazz musician was at the Royal Academy. Joan taught when we were first married, at Morpeth. She'd come from London, she went to Bristol University. Our son and his friend wrote music for a TV documentary about students' grants, 'Taken for Granted'. We've three children and four grandchildren. Our oldest daughter is collections director for a museum. She was a classicist, then organised exhibitions. She's a singer too. She's married to a rector. Our younger daughter did history at university. She went into PR, a small local agency then a bigger UK and US firm. Took a career break, went round the world, then became Corporate PR Manager for a big company in London. One step below the board. She has a baby now so is just getting back to her career.

During this time, Joan constantly took our cups out and washed them, picked things up and moved them about, keeping busy. She then began some serious 'sundowning' type behaviour, putting her coat on again, getting her bag, and saying she had to go to the University to 'sign on', this time she wouldn't be put off. We went outside with her and I asked her to show me the animals and garden, which she did, and we walked all round their house, then we went back in.

David said he sometimes gives lunch parties for understanding friends. Joan goes to Hexham to a Chrysalis Group, has been four times, to paint and draw.

When I left Joan hugged me, they both invited me to come again. During my second visit I saw a copy of Joan's book 'Our Bairns', it was fascinating. I found them very moving as a couple, like so many dealing with this condition, heroic in facing up to it and getting on with it, at a time when they'd have expected some leisure and relaxation.

Earlier painting by Joan

*Recent painting by Joan,
after Alzheimer's*

David and Joan

CHAPTER FOUR
GRAND AND GREAT –
YOUNG PEOPLE ON THEIR SIGNIFICANT ELDERS

HOW YOUNG PEOPLE FEEL ABOUT OLDER
PEOPLE IN THEIR OWN LIVES.

When writing about older people in their own lives and families, there was a marked difference in attitude from the negative stereotypes in Chapter One. Here's a good example:

GRANDAD
Thomas Collins, Year 7

A is for athletic
L is for loyal
A is for achiever
N is for nice and caring

M is for magical
O is for over competitive
R is for right
P is for planning
E is for encouraging
T is for talking
H is for honest

A very different list of adjectives to those previously listed!

Caring for grandchildren or younger family members is yet another vital way older people contribute to society. These pieces show how central to many families this role still is.

Grandparents were described in a loving, even sentimental way, in fact the school students, from Years Seven and Ten, were much more sentimental than the older people I interviewed. Their grandparents were usually described very much in terms of what they do for their grandchildren! Apart from a bit of extra spoiling and sweets, it's clear that many of these grandparents are spending time, and probably money, looking after their grandchildren, helping to raise them, giving them one-to-one time and attention and cooking for them, taking them out and doing activities with them, presumably also helping their children by doing so, either to work, or to have more leisure, or both.

As I've said in my Introduction, I can only hypothesise that the media are bombarding the young with negative stereotypes which do not match their own experiences.

Here are some loving tributes from Year Seven school students.

MY NANA
Emily Jane Thielmann

I love my nana loads and loads, I have loads of great memories with her but these were my favourites . . . . . .
. . . . . My nana used to always take me to Whitehouse Farm; we'd stroke and feed the animals but always the rabbits and horses. We used to ride the tractors and always sat at the front. Me and her would make some multi-coloured candles, to give to my mum, dad and family, she used to buy me a gift for my cousins, and at the end I would want my face painted. I would always get the same style, it was called the ice-princess. But now I don't ever want to go to the farm, so instead she takes my little cousins that do the same as we used to. She gives me and my cousins £5 a week, when we go for our tea every other Monday, and we go shopping on a Friday. She's always offering us money but

I say no. Her husband who is my granddad works away so she gets lonely, and visits lots.

When she goes I will miss her loads, so I wish she will never go, I would miss her hugs, the touch of her hand and her voice that comforts me when I am down. I would visit her grave as often as I could, bringing her favourite flowers, soft sweet smelling purple lavender.

MY GRANDAD

Molly Eve Foxcroft

My favourite memory with me and my Grandad before he died was when it was Christmas and he and my Nanna came over from Barrow.

My mum and my Nanna made turkey with stuffing and it smelt amazing, the smell would remind you of a professional restaurant kitchen it was so good.

We would finish our food and then we would go out for a long walk with the family dog to have a nice chat and it would normally be me, my mum, my dad, my brother, my Nanna and my Grandad. But I and my Grandad didn't feel like it. We stayed in and he gave me a special Christmas present that he didn't tell my brother about. He gave me a little box that was all neatly wrapped up with Rudolph wrapping paper. I was only nine at the time so I liked that sort of stuff.

I opened the box slowly and inside was a game of jacks. Me and him played for hours and never got bored of it. My Grandad was a nice man; he would always wear his long trousers with a fancy jumper and shirt underneath. He loved a cup of tea, so now I know where I get it from as I love tea.

Making each child feel special... and being ditched when they become too 'cool' to hang out with you. Here's a still older generation, still helping out:

GREAT GRANDMA :)

Josh Mayne

My Great Grandma is 95 and amazing, she rushes to help as often as possible. She lived through two world wars and remarkably she is still standing today.

She lives in sheltered housing. Every day she gets the bus with all of her friends and visits the high street to get her daily shopping, leaving at 9am and coming home at 10am and still has the energy to live through the day.

MY GRANDMA

Lewis Denley

My Grandma is always there to help out even if it is hard for her. She makes me laugh and smile when I'm sad or hurt. She knows me so well as she always gets my favourite sweets. She works so hard for me to be happy that the least I can do is laugh and smile. She knows so much and is always interested in my day at school. She encourages me to do my best in all subjects and is very responsible. My Grandma can drive which is a great bonus for getting around. I love going to her house for Sunday lunch because it is the nicest I have ever had.

MY GRANDMA

Millie Elsdon

The smell of her perfume drifted up my nose
To me and my friends, she owned a lot of strange clothes

She may have been loopy and eccentric at times,
She always used to make up rhymes,
About when she was a girl, when the world was fine
And just how different her childhood was to mine!

'C'mon poppet heart,' she'd shout up the stairs
I'd run as fast as I could, leaving a trail of teddy bears
She'd walk me along to the nearest bus stop
But we wouldn't just walk, we'd always hop
Dancing and humming, to a recognised tune
She'd always repeat 'we'll be there soon.'

The bus would arrive with time to spare,
So she'd buy me some sweeties, to show she cared
She'd pull out some tissues from her bag,
'Wipe your nose and quit being a drag,'
She'd nag me and nag me, over again,
Sometimes I'd say 'Grandma, you're going insane.'

However being my Grandma, she'll always know,
I will never stop loving her so!

MY GRANDMA
Ewan Pearson

My grandma is the kindest person I've ever met. She's always there if me and my brother need looking after and always spoils us. She always has her hair in a high white curly bun and always wears a bright top and jeans. Her and my granddad cook the most delicious meals of spaghetti bolognese and Sunday lunch.

MY GRANDDAD
Andrew Mather

My granddad is always rushing to help. He makes me laugh and I've had a lot of great times with them. I could say I look up to him because when he was my age he was a lot like me. He always tries to help me whenever I need it. He is very knowledgeable and always has something kind to say. My granddad makes me laugh and smile and he is very fun. Before he had to go to the hospital he would come round and take my dog for a walk. He is always interested in what's been happening to me and always asks me questions about football, school etc. He and my grandma spoil me too much I think because they have a special sweet drawer for me and my sisters. My granddad always wears a shirt and school type trousers and always sits in his favourite armchair in the corner of the room. Sadly my granddad is in the hospital because of heart problems, however I think he will be fine because he always thinks on the bright side and always seems to be happy!

MY NANA

Stephanie Gardner

Love and warmth fill her heart
She pushes round her shopping cart
Looking around the shopping mart
She works for free and does her part
Her mind remains as sharp as a dart.

Although she's old, and wrinkly too!
And she's completely hopeless with all things new
She loves me for me, no matter who.
When I was young she told me cows go "moo,"
"Come on my darling," she'd coo.

She always smells of fresh soap
She wraps her arms around me like a rope
And whenever I was in a mope
She told me that I'd cope
And she fills my heart with hope.

MY GRANDMA

Ben McGee

My grandma is simply amazing. She's kind, funny and is always there whenever I need her. Somehow she manages to cope with me, my two brothers and my two cousins all at the same time. Her and my grandad make the best curry and my favourite Sunday lunch. She always wears a dress with a cardigan on top. She has black, curly hair.

Food, food, and more food! But the fun of cooking too. Aunts can be 'great' too!

MY GREAT AUNTY

Lucy Sloan

I had a great aunty,
We used to go everywhere,
From farm to farm, uphill and home,
We never had time to spare.

I had a great aunty,
The stories she would tell,
Were filled with joy and happiness,
Her book, you couldn't sell.

I had a great aunty,
Her home would welcome you in,
It was filled with things that had been passed down,
And the corridors were thin.

I had a great aunty,
I loved the sweetie drawer,
I used to decorate shortbread sticks,
And spill icing on the floor.

Now some grandparent stories from Year Ten students.

Looking at the Year Ten pieces after Year Seven, it appears that those three extra years give a new perspective. Some of the pieces are in the past tense: the deaths of grandparents are often a child's first personal experience of death, apart from pets'. There is an added distance too, the sentimental love and appreciation of being spoiled is now enriched by a greater awareness of faults or quirks, and also of the legacy they have passed on, in appearance, or gifts or interests. The beginning of teenage 'judging' of elders is here, and disapproval of bad habits like smoking.

MY GRAMPA
Louise Nicholls

William Stonehouse Garfitt was my grampa. He sadly died at the ripe age of 71. When he gave you a hug there was the fresh aroma of freshly cut grass mixed with a sweet smell of roses. He dressed in very similar clothes each day. He wore a cap, shirt and black or navy pants with a huge creamy white jacket. My gramps loved all his grandchildren, I was his favourite.

My grampa took us out every Saturday and Sunday. In the car we always listened to my grampa's favourite music. ABBA and the Beach Boys, he always called me Chiquitita, his favourite ABBA song. He took us anywhere we wanted. He even said that if he could he would take us to the moon. My grampa always reminded me of a big huggable bear. He was great to hug, it felt like hugging a giant beanbag.

My gramps enjoyed gardening (I think some of his gardening skills have had an effect on me). The last few months of his life, I hated. Seeing him hooked up to all sorts of machines, every time I saw him I wanted to cry. Even though he was very tired, he still had the energy to comfort me and tell me everything will be alright.

I remember the last thing he ever said to me. 'Louise, you remind me of a beautiful crimson rose, all dark and mysterious at first, but then blossoming into a beautiful young lady. I'm so proud of you. Never forget that and when

I'm gone and you feel lonely, just look up at the night sky and see me shining back at you.'

My grampa loved being in the great outdoors. Every day he would be out in the garden looking after his precious flowers. I've still got the beautiful iris plant he gave me. It's a shame he never got to see them blossom. They're beautiful, white with a blob of purple bleeding into the white. My mam says she sees so much of him in me. He was a very positive man always smiling never shouting, the perfect grampa.

GRANDA

Elliot Patterson

My granda who passed away a couple of months ago was 87 when he died and he was called Ken 'Elliot' Muir, where I got my first name from. He was always strong physically and mentally. He always used to love to build stuff in his house and outside in the garden. He also used to build ships in the war or WWII for the British navy. He used to love people to go round to his house because his wife, my nana, died when I was five years old so he has no-one to talk to and he used to go on and on about what was going on in his life. We could never get him to shut up!

GRANDDAD

Joseph Monaghan

My granddad is 68. He always takes me out in the summer holidays and he always has time for me. Whenever he visits me he always smells of oil because he is always fixing his motorbike. A happy time I had with him was when he took me to Scotland to watch a bike race and he slipped down a hill. A bad time was when I went to a fayre with him and I got lost and I couldn't find him and when I eventually did find him he cried because he didn't think he was ever going to find me. The colour red reminds me best of him because he has two red motorbikes and he is always cleaning them. Foods that remind me of him are jelly and Bassets liquorice allsorts. The drink that reminds me of him is a cup of tea. My granddad is always fixing his motorbikes even if they don't need fixing.

GRANDMA

Hannah Richardson

My grandma lives in a bungalow with my granddad. She is quite small and hunches over slightly. She always wears t shirts and black pants. She mostly goes shopping in Marks and Spencer and John Lewis. She has a short sharp grey bob. She is wrinkly and is quite tanned. She always wears slippers around the house, but is quite active. She sees her friends a lot, goes on walks, goes to town but always stays local. She is not as active as she used to be because she had a heart operation at Christmas time but is slowly recovering. She is a very stubborn woman set in her ways and usually thinks her way is the best way. The bungalow in which she lives is quite modern and she keeps it immaculate always. It smells of something fresh but not strong. She loves her plants so keeps a nice garden full of lots of flowers and has a pond with frogs. She doesn't watch TV very much and reads a lot. Usually she reads a thick book a week, and reads the same kinds of books like detective books. She always gets up very early in the morning and goes to bed quite early.

I REMEMBER

Bethany Johnson

It's a long time ago, but I remember you,
We used to play dominos cause it's what you loved to do,
You wore slippers, stockings and used curlers in your hair,
You always were smiling in your little red chair,
You always smelled fresh and loved boiled sweets,
If you beat me at cards you'd pay me back with treats.
I always think of you as a caring happy soul,

You didn't have many wrinkles even though you were old.
You liked to eat oranges and watch war videos,
You had white hair and I got my brown eyes off you,
You've always been caring, and a crease, too!

MY AUNTIE

Grant Wilkinson

85 years old. Blonde. Blue eyes. That's her in a nutshell. She watches everything on the TV, all the soaps.

Her house always (nearly always) smells of smoke. I think it's embedded in the wallpaper (probably why it's slightly yellow instead of white) even though she says she hasn't smoked in years.

She also loves her food: chocolates, sweets, cakes and everything else. The whole family know this and that's why Thorntons do a good trade every Christmas. You can see the pile of chocolate boxes growing as the 25th December rolls on. But by the end of January, about half of these boxes are in our food cupboards (she probably gets sickened with them...but I'm not complaining.)

She hasn't got very good hearing. You could say, deaf. Not deaf enough to watch TV with subtitles, but enough to have the volume above the level safe for human ears.

GRANDDAD

Bradley Wailes

My granddad, old but fun, spends his life at the local pub. Cards is his game... he plays every weekend with his friends. He retired from being a police dog trainer (which I've heard plenty about) and now he still works part time but as a carpenter down at the local woodyard. Although I've told him many times, he still smokes quite a bit and has the occasional cigar. He used to be in the navy and loves everything blue, he owns a navy blue cardigan that's always smelling of smoke.

MY NANA

Megan Atkinson

The heating is always on in her house, so it is always super hot.
She will not let me leave the house until I have eaten something.
My nana always has a glass of white wine or a cup of tea out of a green mug
whilst sitting on a green leather sofa.
I look like my nana, however she is wrinkly.
At 2pm she sits and eats a salad that she doesn't like but forces herself to eat.
She shops at New Look and goes to keep fit.

GRANDDAD

Ryan Chan

My granddad is old but active. He has a hobby of going to the casino a lot. He
dresses relatively smartly with a light coloured jacket and pants. He walks
slowly with either a cigar in his mouth or a packet in his coat pocket. When I
was young he would look after me when my parents went to work or went out.
My granddad is very active and loves to cook. He makes the most of when his
grandchildren come to visit, he is always very happy.

There was only one negative grandparent piece, about a very distant, little known
grandparent from another culture. And this one, an observation:

ANGRY MAN

Andrew Weeks

The year below me were playing football across the street from the bus stop I
was waiting at after school. They accidentally kicked the football into a garden
and a man came out, calm and quiet, picked up the football and threw it...
away from them. He appeared to be angry and alone with his god seeming to

be his only companion. No wonder he feels isolated with an attitude like that.

An interesting perspective. The gulf between the old and the young who are strangers to each other is as sad, as the special relationship between the old and the young who are close, is heartening.

CHAPTER FIVE
LIVING HISTORY, LIVING HERSTORY

As well as finding out about what older people are doing now, I learned a great deal about what they did in the past, that 'other country' which seems so alien to modern children. We learn the history of Kings and Queens and battles, but what of the lives of working class men and women, and of the children they were? These contributors speak of long ago children's games, large families, poverty eased by love and imagination, in very different times to our own. But history goes in cycles, not straight lines, so who knows when we may need to relearn how to live like this again?

DAISY, 96
Tells of rural life before taps, toilets and electricity: family fun and tragedy, and her mam, who made nightdresses for the dead. (AC Centre)

I'm nearly 96. I can remember back to when there was no gas, no electricity, no water, and no flushing toilets in our houses! For toilets, there was a place outside, a hole, with a plank across it with a hole in it, you sat on there and it all went down into the hole, which had ash from the fire in it. When it got too full, the night soil men came round and shovelled it out and took it away.

I grew up in the little village of Lanchester. My first important memory, was when I was four, September 28th. My little brother died, he was just two years ten months old. He'd always been a weakly boy, his chest it was. In fact I remember when I was about two, my auntie giving him to me to nurse. I loved him and helped to look after him. This day, I'd been to Sunday school, and I came home, and all the blinds were drawn. I didn't understand it, as I opened the door, I yelled, 'what's wrong in here?' A lady said, 'be quiet, Daisy! I'll take you to our house, I've got some special biscuits just for you, custard creams.' And she took me to her daughter's house. They were great Methodists, and we were Church of England, but we were very very friendly with them. Her daughter fed me with custard creams and told me a story, of how our Thomas had died, and what it meant, about what death was. I said, you go to chapel, and we go to church, you say god means no harm, so why should god take my brother away? I said I wasn't going to church again! I didn't for a long time. My father said, leave her alone, she'll come round on her own. In fact later on I went to chapel instead of church. My father's father died in his 80s, that was the next time I came near death. I said then, if god lets us live a long time, he's sorry that he took my brother. No, I didn't see my little brother after he died, and I didn't go to the funeral, but I knew where he was buried, and when I was old enough to walk through the village on my own, I'd pick daisies and buttercups and put them on his grave.

I was the eldest, and I had a sister and two brothers, including Thomas. My father was a blacksmith, I thought he was very clever. He shod horses. I used to watch him do it, cut bits off a long piece of iron, put them in the fire until they were red hot, soft enough to hammer into horse shoe shapes, then he'd plunge them into water to cool them. But they were still hot when he put them onto the horse's hoof. I'd ask question after question, why does the horse stand and let you do that with hot iron? But it's like your fingernail, where the hot iron goes. When the old shoes had worn through, he'd take them off and trim the hoof and nail the new ones on. That went on for years. Everybody had a horse! There were no buses, you walked everywhere. There was a railway line, from Durham City to Black Hill, it ran at 8 in the morning and at 5 at night, because Dorman and Long of Middlesbrough were building Consett Ironworks. But on Saturday, there was a train at noon as well, there and back. The engine would turn round on a turntable.

Water supply, well we had a tap, outside, which lots of houses shared. It was a pump at first, then later a modern pipe with a tap on the top, about a foot off the ground. No water in the house. Then later, when I was nine I think, we got drains dug underground. Before that, you had a bucket under the sink, all the slops went in there and then your dad took it out and threw it in the netty!

Lighting, we had candles, always on a saucer filled with water. Then some oil was produced for oil lamps, a big iron tank on a horse-drawn wagon brought it. We had coal fires, but only in the kitchen, it was like a kitchen range, with an oven on one side, the fire in the middle, and on the other side a place to heat water. We used a tin bath, my mother would heat water, and we'd use it one at a time! They added more hot water between us, but didn't empty any. Dad had a bath in the back kitchen. Or a wash, he'd wash as far up as he could then sit on a stool with his feet in the bowl. But we didn't have the colds and flu then! To keep warm in bed, we'd steal a brick from a building site, put it in the oven, wrap in an old blanket, and put it in the bed.

I went to the village school, age 5-7 in a cloakroom, 7-11 in the Sunday school place, and a bit was taken off that to make a room for the 11-14. Very very few sat exams for the grammar school. When you started you had a slate, and a slate pencil to write on it with, which was another piece of slate. You didn't get a real pencil or paper until they were sure you could write properly with the slate pencil. We learned the alphabet and numbers, and had to write 'the cat sat on the mat', and we read the bible. We had no story books. I loved school, my mother believed in teaching, she was better than the teachers, she helped me. My mam kept house, she had to do a lot of housework and also walking to both sets of grandparents, my father's parents lived at Greencroft, Anfield Plain, and my mother's parents lived at Consett. Before she married, when she was 33, which is why she only had four children, she was a dressmaker and tailoress. So she made all our clothes, beautifully embroidered, she was very clever. She made 'laying out nighties' for persons who had died in the area. They were made of very fine calico called 'lawn', long sleeves, all buttoned up to the neck, they fastened all the way up the front, each side was beautifully embroidered with white silk. A woman used to lay out the dead. Mrs Bainbridge. She brought people into the world, and she saw them out! She was the cleverest woman in the village. I used to go to my grandparents in the summer holidays. When we got back to school, the teacher would ask, what did you do on your summer holidays? This one year, I was about ten, my next little brother was born in the holidays. So when the teacher asked, I stood up, I remember as clear as crystal, and said, 'I had a baby boy!' it didn't take long for that to go right round the village. Boys at school teased me about it, but I said, Mrs Bainbridge said, 'here's your baby, you look after it', and she always tells the truth! So it was definitely 'my' baby! He was born in the night, in the morning they said, have you seen what you've got? I helped Mam look after him. We were very happy, we all helped each other. Our parents were very kind, even my father. We were known in the village as a wonderful family, we were taught proper manners, and how to talk properly. My mother's mother had terrible rheumatism, she could just get from chair to table to chair, she was never known to go out of the house except when my father borrowed a pony and trap and went to collect her, and brought her to our house for a holiday. My grandpa looked after her usually, everyone round there helped him, because he'd do anything for anyone and was always helping people. And he could cook as well as any woman.

At 14, I left school, and was kept at home to learn to bake, cook, and all housekeeping jobs. When I was 18 I started nursing, our doctor was making his surgery into a hospital, and I started there, helping him. I worked from 7.30 in the morning til 8.30 at night. I was determined to work until I got £5 a week! Well I went to chapel and there were plenty of chapel lads for me, all in St John Ambulance, and I met my husband through them, when I was 22. We were engaged for years. I was paid monthly, so the minute I got £5 a week, my husband said, that's it, put your month's notice in! And we got married. He was a miner. But studying hard to be a colliery manager. He was 3 days too old to apply for help from the miners, so he says, I'll do it on me own! And he did. It was hard work. A correspondence course as well as working as a miner. He said, I've paid for two years just to look at a different lot of grass, and learn how earth was formed.

We had one son. Only the one, the doctor said I mustn't have any more. I was very ill, had an awful nine months, it was touch and go we'd both live. When I was having him, they wanted to fetch my husband home from the pit as I was going to die, but I said, no, let him work, he'll be all dirty from the pit anyway, by the time he'd washed it off... but I didn't die. I think it was because I prayed. My son was a little scratty thing! When he was over 2 month old, his dad watched me bath him, and he said then, you're wasting your time. I said, don't you dare say that again, he'll have to survive. I've always said it was prayer that saved him. And my nursing experience. He's a fine man now! He's a professional chef. I made his wedding anniversary card here this morning, he's going to be 27years married this Saturday. He has no children, and that's a sore point, because he loves children, but it just didn't happen. He lives south of York, he visits when he can.

I live in my own bungalow, I had a stroke so we got the bungalow, about twenty four year ago. My husband died nine years ago. He was a wonderful husband. We had a wonderful happy life. We worked hard and saved hard, but by crumbs did we enjoy it!

My advice, take the old fashioned ways, be more content with what you've got, and do not want to be better than the woman next door! But it's wonderful what they can do now, I saw this week they've given new hearts to two babies.

BETH, 82
A skilled baker, with vivid memories of long ago children's games, mischief in the tough city streets. (DCP Centre)

DCP have a policy of encouraging people with dementia to do things at the Centres, to help maintain their skills. I watched Beth baking scones and fruitcake, and cleaning up afterwards. When she came to sit down, I asked her about baking.

BETH'S STORY.
I baked bread, cakes, scones, pastry. The secret's in the lightness of your hands. If you do it lightly, you get things to rise. I like bread buns best, once they've cooled, with strawberry jam. My two girls went to the Tyneside Theatre every Saturday, my brother worked there, he'd give them ice creams. I used to bake til they came back, then they'd have their tea. They learned from watching me, I'd talk to them all the time. I used to knit a lot as well. My youngest, she'd go to sleep to the sound of the needles clicking. Once for Easter I made them polka dot cardigans, I'd finished one, nearly finished the other. An old man with no

telly, I'd let him watch the football on ours so he brought me a Guiness, and it got knocked over on the cardigan! I got it all out in cold water, dried it and it was ready for Easter Sunday.

Childhood games? We used to play with top and whips, I liked that. You put your knee on top, pulled the whip, and the top would spin away! We'd put boody, coloured paper, on the tops, see who had the bonniest. Ah, we got our summers then! Tar on the road would melt and bubble, we'd burst the bubbles and use margarine to get it off our hands. We played skippies. Parents would come out and turn the rope sometimes. 'Tin the Block'; I was a dab hand at that! You had an empty tin upside down, four sticks on top, two teams trying to knock the sticks off with a ball. 'Cowboys and Indians', we'd play, we'd hide in folks' washhouses. And Saturday nights, at Cockburn's Fruit Shop, we'd climb over the wall and get the left over fruit. We left nowt! We saved the bin men a canny job! Oh it was lovely. Those little green seedless grapes! They're lovely with crushed walnuts. We'd share the fruit, there was all sorts. And we pinched rhubarb from an allotment and dipped it in Mam's sugar, we'd get a belly ache next day. One day me dad came with a spoon of medicine for the belly ache, he give us the medicine then he whacked my leg, saying, 'don't ever do that again, if I ever find out you've pinched from that allotment woe betide you my lady!' So I stopped. We played 'Knocky Nine Doors'. Women would come out, 'did you see anybody at the door?' But we helped old people then, my mam made us go and ask them, if they wanted any housework done or anything, you had to do it! I had two fights at school. One for my sister and one for my friend. I fought other girls from the tanyard slums, dickies in their heads, no knickers. Oh, when you fight for your own, you fight hard. I got the belt, once. And once, me and another girl were crawling down the school stairs, the teacher says, 'if you behave like animals, we'll treat you like animals', she got the older girls to make paper tails and pin them on us, we had to wear them for two days!

And dolls! We had baby dolls, me and me sisters would go to my gran's, she lived next door, and knit baby clothes for them. One day the priest came. We'd all been christened at his church, all nine of us. I was 3 or 4. He had two shoeboxes with him. He opened one, it had a lovely doll, all in lemon. He give it to our Bronwen. He give me the other, it was a black doll! I'd never seen a darkie doll before. I'd only ever seen one black man, who came with a suitcase every fortnight with scarves to sell. And I said to the priest, 'I don't want that one, it's dirty!' My mother said, 'I could've killed you! I wished the ground had swallowed me.' But this doll was beautiful, she had gold earrings, bangles, a turban, a flared 3 colour dress, me dad put it on the sideboard and I'd keep looking at it. One day my sister got it down and give it me. I loved it then! Well one day I was rocking my baby doll in my arms and I smashed her head on the iron, I was crying and crying, my dad said he'd try and fix it. I went to bed still crying, I heard my brother come in from courting, I asked him to look and see if it was mended, he says, yes, so I got up and had a peep, he'd papered her head! With sticky paper! And my sister'd knitted a hat to go over the paper. I was thrilled to bits!

I'm 82. What do I think of being young then? It was brilliant, there was no TV, you had your own imagination, you could be anybody, you could do anything, it was better to be young then. We were happy. Grown -ups had time for children then. You don't see them give a bairn a penny now! We'd copy the films, you'd be Shirley Temple. You couldn't do that now, there'd be nobody left alive!

AUTHOR'S NOTE: Beth's reaction to the black doll made me think, how at that time the north east was almost entirely white, but men with black faces were a common sight in a region famous for coalmining – children would see the miners walking home with their faces totally black with coal dust, no wonder children associated black faces with dirt. Yet even today there are few black dolls around, whereas Beth was given one back then. Beth also retains her skills in baking today, and is aware of modern films and how violent they are.

ANNIE

Despite childhood brain damage, still bright at 87, with wartime stories
and how family love eased childhood poverty. (AL SOC Centre)

My father was in the Boer war! Yes, the Boer war. Then he went to Canada, he
was a Mountie! I had wonderful parents. Lovely. There were seven of us, we
always had lovely clothes. Me mother was spotless. We were all well brought
up. She worked hard until late at night, like a little doll of a woman she was. She
had to wash our pants and socks every night, all seven of us, every night, because
we only had one set each! We had to go to Sunday school every week, but we
had to take our glad rags off when we got home! Oh, dear, if you got a hole in
anything -! My father was a labourer in the boneyard at Walker Road, St
Anthony's. We used to make hooky mats and clippy mats. We had a wood frame,
with sacking, like hessian across, we'd hook bits of material from old clothes
through it to make rugs. Hooky, you'd weave the strips of material in and out,
clippie, you'd cut it into short lengths and hook them through and tie them so
you got a rug with a pile.

I used to play with a girl from up the road, she was filthy. She had dickies,
she was walkin'! My mam didn't like me playing with her but she was my friend
and I loved her. Her mam worked in the fish and chip shop, but mam made us
throw away the free chips we got! But it wasn't her fault. She was my friend.
Oh, she was clever, she passed for a scholarship to the grammar school – I didn't,
I was dense! Well she got cleaner when she had to go there, I think she realised
and kept herself clean. I think some other people in her family helped her with
the uniform. I wasn't good at school. I was run over and nearly killed when I
was little. By a boy on a bike! I saw somebody across the road and ran across
just as he came along going fast, the pedal went right into my head! I had a hole
in it! Look, it's flat!

(AUTHOR'S NOTE: She shows me her right temple or a bit higher, it's oddly
flat and like a piece of bone had been shaved off under the skin.)

They thought I would die. I was in hospital for ages. When I got home I was in a cot in case I got bumped. I've got brain damage. People came round with sweets, I was spoiled! Yes, I nearly died, but I'm still here and I'm 87! All seven of us did well for ourselves. I've a brother who was a foreman at Swan's. My first job was in the jam factory and then an ammunition factory in Newcastle. I was sent to Birmingham, we had to sit at tables in the aircraft hangars and check everything. I was courting my husband at the time. There were Americans in Birmingham, oh they were after us, all the bonny lasses! And lovely young pilots! Our landlady would come to the pub and sit with us as a chaperone. We had lemonade shandy. But the landlord was a beady fellow. He used to… we didn't like him. I told my husband and he said 'right, come home and marry me.' He was handsome, six foot two. He was lovely. He worked with my brother in the shipyard. My brother went in the navy but my husband had to stay in the shipyards, they needed men there. We had a white wedding in Byker parish church, I was 20. He used to play the accordion and the piano. But he got ill and died. He got like a skeleton. It was his lungs. I think they breathed in all sorts at the shipyard. I had four children, three girls and a boy. My son's in Cyprus, he worked in the oil fields in Saudi then he moved to Cyprus. But he came straight over when I was ill! My three daughters come turn and turn about through the week to see me. Take me out for runs in the car. We go down to Cullercoats for breakfast! We used to go there as bairns. One of my sons in law's father was harbour master there. All four of my bairns did well, all have their own houses. I still live in my council house, it suits me. My neighbour's 90, when they arrived they had nowt, pushing a cart, but they did well. My mam said poor people do better because they push harder.

My great grandson is 3. He comes in my house, I have to turn away, he's so funny! He talks posh, we don't know where he gets it. He says 'mee' instead of 'mih'.

So, I've had a good life. A lovely family. I've brought up my children. We all help each other. I used to get terrible headaches with my brain damage, but I don't get so many now. They're really bad but I don't mind, as long as I'm still here! I come here Saturday and Sunday, I see the family through the week, they're all lovely.

AUTHOR'S NOTE: Annie used lots of family names (which I've omitted) without stumbling. She repeated bits of the story several times, but not more than a lot of people do. She seemed very bright despite her brain injury. I noticed she'd put her hand to her temple when she was trying to remember something. She was very lively. Both she and her friend were very neat, clean, with hair immaculate, they get carers in all day with meals etc and lots of nearby family support.

VIOLET PEART, 96

A hard but happy life, now an enthusiastic queen look-alike! A beautiful scene of her and her sisters bathing her mother, all talking and laughing together. (AC Centre)

Violet is tiny, thin, with misty spectacles especially one lens which is frosted, a tight neat perm and dangly diamond earrings. She almost immediately got some photographs out of her handbag to show me, pictures of her in fancy dress as the Queen.

VIOLET'S STORY:

That's me in the photos! I've always been a person who dresses up, all me life. So in 1977, I organised our street party for the Queen's Jubilee. I dressed as the Queen, I made the dress meself, out of cellophane. That's how it started. One day I was dressed as the Queen, a chap came through, from St Michaels, Heaton Road. He says, will you come and open a place for us?! So I opened a new centre at Walker Road, dressed as the Queen, in June 1994. The Lord Mayor was there: the children presented me with a bouquet. We had a lovely do! I just dress up for the fun of it. I made that crown in the photo. I've had five of them! They get bashed about you know. No, I've not met the real Queen, I've met Princess Ann though. I'm 96, now, I've got no social worker or carers, I'm losing the sight in one eye and the other has double vision, I feel lost, I sit in the house all day when I'm not here at the day centre once a week, or at a lunch club for me lunch once a week. Yes I'm slim now, I used to be ten stone, I'm shrinking!

Oh, I've had a wonderful life. I had twins! And I had a good husband, bless him, he died when he was 63. We looked forward to our retirement, he never got it. He was a good lad. He loved his bingo, but I hated it. It's boring! He died of cancer. He smoked you know. I got a lovely single bed for him, so I'd not disturb him while he was ill, but he wouldn't sleep in it, he came back to our bed. I never bothered with anyone else. We had a caravan at Hexham, we used to go there every weekend. Well I worked for 54 year, for a man from the Co-op. His wife tret me like a daughter. I cleaned for them. He was manager of the pharmacy. She was a lovely woman, she'd say, 'sit down and tell me a tale.' I've got two grandchildren, and five great grandchildren. I had twin boys, but I lost one at 34. He dropped down dead, he had a brain tumour he didn't know about. But the other twin become more like the one who died, who bossed him about! They had mops of curly hair. One was more like me, boisterous, the other quiet, like my husband. I met my husband when he was playing football for a local team, I used to go and watch. His brother played for Everton! He was killed playing, hit his head.

I'm one of ten children, four boys and six girls. My father was the strictest you ever knew. But as we grew older, we realised he was a wonderful man – none of his six daughters had to get married! He showed photos of us to everyone. My mother never once lost her temper. She'd just say, 'I'll tell your dad.' He never did hit us, but he'd get the belt out and show us it! We were frightened of him, we thought he was horrible when we were young, but he was a good dad. Me mother was funny. When she was old, we'd go down, all six of us sisters, and bath her. She'd say, 'why do I need all these?' My youngest sister would get in with her and hold her, and we'd all wash her, and we'd all be giggling and talking, me mother and her six daughters, all together.

AUTHOR'S NOTE, March 2011: Violet has since died. Her description of the six sisters bathing their mother, laughing and talking together, moves me deeply and makes me smile every time I read it.

JANE AND NELL

Tales of the past, 'possing' and poverty. (AL SOC)

Nell is good humoured, seeming 'normal', Jane more random and a little confused in her speech though lively in style.

NELL'S STORY.

I lived in Spital Tongues, went to school there. Then Todd's Nook. I was born at The Dwellings. It was a cold place then, all black, the (coal) dirt made the stone black. There was a fish shop and a little corner shop, Bennet's. Mabel worked there for years, (Note: others remembered Mabel, clearly a local character) she was old as the hills. And there was a newspaper shop opposite the bus stop. My dad worked in New Bridge Street, I can't seem to remember what he did. My mother was an upholstress. She worked for a shop called Curtains, on Northumberland Street, she made curtains and covers for three piece suites, with the piping on the edges and all that. She worked at home, there was sewing everywhere! There was only me and my brother at home. Have you ever seen a poss tub?

(poss tub: used before washing machines: a tub, and a pole with a three-pronged wooden 'stool' on the end, which was used to bash and swirl the clothes in the tub.)

I remember my grandma and I had a go at it. When I got a job we sat at high tables with a bar under that you put your feet on. I worked in High Friars Street. I can't quite say what I did.

NOTE: Nell has a reputation for being good with numbers, the staff thought she'd worked in the tax office. She seemed good at remembering street names, rather than jobs.

JANE'S STORY.

I was born on City Road, in the back lane. It was a going place – it had four pubs, shops, a wash house. Did we have to take our washing there? Well they weren't going to bring the water to your house were they pet! (*to staff member who'd asked the question.*)

Poss tubs, well I was level with the top when I was possing. I'm little now so you can imagine how small I was then. I was below all the mothers. They wondered what the noise was! I was one of seven children. Father worked in the shipyard, people think they had money but we didn't. My hair was golden red then, long down my back. Bits would be curling out and all over the place, my mam'd say, 'come here, I'll take you to my mother's', and then she'd pull me to bits! She'd say 'eeh that bairn', and take me to A E Booths (*later she told this story again and said A E Cooks*). She took me down there and they took my clothes off, I was screaming blue murder, I thought she might leave me there like that! But I got all rigged out, in new clothes, when they told me grandma it was so much, she said 'What! I could make better meself!' Though I never saw her sew. When I got home my mam said 'eeh, I cannot afford that, you'll have to take it back.' But my grandma would help her out with money if she had any. I was named after my grandma, and I had to go round there and sleep with her in the same bed. I was forced to, she'd send for me at nights though we lived in another house. She'd make me wash my hands and face. Looking back, she was good to me. But she'd tell me what to do and what I could have.

CHAPTER SIX
THE BAD OLD DAYS: SURVIVORS OF ABUSE

Strong family and community bonds helped people cope with poverty and bereavement and any problems life brought them.

But it's worth remembering, when people talk of family values, what that meant for some people, women and children in particular, who often endured decades of domestic violence or sexual abuse with no hope of escape, either within the family, or in institutions and orphanages. Yet all those whose stories follow below, have survived, bloody but unbowed, having brought up their children or otherwise lived productive lives, and often have a happier life now in their old age than they did as young people.

EILEEN, 78
Happy at last, though disabled, after a 58 year violent abusive marriage,
a busy work life nursing, and bringing up five children. (AC Centre)

I've been in this wheelchair four years now. I want to tell you, I'm married, it would be 60 years, but after 58 years I'd had enough, and left him! He was horrible. I'm a different person now! I've a beautiful flat. Self-contained. Carers come in and help me get up and dress and get my meals. I've a lovely view, you'll laugh when I tell you what it is – a Working Mens' Club! Well there's a lot going on, you get a great view especially from up a height.

My husband? He looked down on me and said things like, when I was on crutches, 'Time you were in your box'. Kept telling me I knew nowt. He was a clever man, mind. I was seven year younger. And he'd hit me – his favourite place was the back of my neck, oh he was too canny – the bruises didn't show there. And after he'd done it, he'd deny it! Truth is, I was frightened of him. I'd wait for him coming in from drinking with his mates every night, wondering what sort of mood he'd be in. And he'd never apologise for anything. He just thought of himself, even with our five children. He was nasty to them as well. Why did I put up with it for 58 years, well you did in those days. Somehow I didn't realise, well I was fed up for years, even the family said to leave, but I didn't know how, who was going to keep me? Where would I go? Sometimes he'd be very loving, but you never knew when he'd go the other way.

So, I was on crutches, before I was in this chair all the time, and I got a urinary infection, gave me hallucinations, all sorts, I was in a terrible way. I got taken into hospital, I was there sixteen weeks. And the staff there were lovely to me! So kind and caring. The way they spoke to me, sort of made me realise how it had been living with him. And yes, that I deserved better. So I decided not to go home. And the staff got the flat for me, and helped me with benefits and carers and so on. I'm very lucky. The doctor said I was very brave. I don't know about that but I had to be strong. You know, since I've left him, my blood pressure's gone down!

People don't put up with things now, don't stay in marriages, they're just off! It's a good thing they can get help. Though people nowadays are less tolerant, they want too much, ready for suing people, and it's all about money nowadays. I didn't tell anybody about my husband before that, I was ashamed. And after 58 years, when I left him, I felt upset, that I'd failed in my marriage. So when I decided to leave him, he was standing in the hospital – he'd visited me three times in three weeks, though it was near – I said, 'I'm not coming home'.

He said, 'What you mean?'

'I'm leaving you.'

'Why wasn't I told?'

'I'm telling you now.'

'Oh.' And he left, and I've never seen him since.

His aunt said he didn't used to be like that, til he fought in the war, and he was never the same after he came back. Just 17 when he went, he came back a different person. He couldn't talk about it, until he was 80, he told me some of it. He was a parachutist, in Greece. He went to a farmhouse, the whole family were sitting round the table, all dead, with their feet blown off. His two pals were killed, either side of him, and him not touched.

I didn't tell my mam and dad about my marriage. I was ashamed. My father was warm and loving, I was closest to him, and I had an uncle who'd make a huge fuss of me, send me presents. Once he sent me a little chair, and a desk, filled with easter eggs! I kept that until about ten years ago. But my mam wasn't loving, especially to me. She didn't want daughters – and she had four, and one son. And he was killed when he was nineteen. On his motorbike. Articulated lorry swung out and killed him. Mam never got over it. She was a woman that disliked herself. My dad died just eight months later, cancer, but I believe the shock did it.

Why do I still wear my rings? D'you know, I bought these myself! Yes, a new wedding ring, and a nice engagement ring, and this other ring, and this nice watch – I bought them all when I'd left him, I had a bit money saved up. I felt guilty but the children said I deserved it, so I treated myself. I'd never had anything nice. My old engagement ring had got sold when we were hard up. My old wedding ring's still in the old house with him. All our children are comfortable now, and I'm better off than when I was married! I'm nearly 79 now, I'd never had a penny from anyone until I left him when I was 76.

I spent twenty year at home bringing up my five children. They're lovely and all have done well. All clever. I've 11 grandchildren, and 8 great-grandchildren. Then I spent twenty one year as a nurse – right here, in this building, when it used to be a premature baby unit! And now I'm here being cared for.
Regrets, well I've only ever had the one man in my life. I get upset on social nights, when I see the old couples happy together, and I wish I could have had that. Something better than what I had. And I'd like to be able to walk. But I'm alive, and my brain's all right.

And I believe, if you're happy, your brain's brighter, you think better. I'm happy now, with nice friends, we've a communal sitting room where I socialise, one of my best friends has both legs taken off, but she's full of fun, and has a nice loving husband. I took up painting when I was 62, we paint on glass, and on silk, and stick jewels on. I make cards. I come here to the Centre one day a week, we do all sorts. The staff here are smashing. I've always knitted, and baked. I watch TV quizzes, I love University Challenge. So I'm happy, and I'm lucky.

DOREEN, 81

A hard life of poverty, unmarried pregnancy, abusive marriage, ill health
and many children, later a new love and religion, now at peace with life.
(AC Centre)

I'm 81. Had a bad life really. But there's been happiness amid the unhappiness.
It all started when I went out with a gang of girls when I was 18. I wasn't used
to that sort of thing. We ended up at the Rex Hotel in Whitley Bay and I met a
lad, I wasn't very keen on him really. I found out he lodged near where I lived.
Me grandma lived with us and said he'd been round asking for me. He'd said,
'feel my beard, I've been working all hours and all night to get a ship finished.'
She passed on the message and he asked me out to the pictures. Couple of nights
later, we went to the cinema and he gave me a box of chocolates. I was
embarrassed, not used to it, but he said, go on, open them! He was Scots.
Anyway, another time I went to meet him with a friend of mine. We all got drunk.
Of course you can guess what happened, I got into trouble. I was pregnant, and
he didn't want anything to do with me, he denied it was his and rejected me. The
Doctor said he'd send a Social Worker round, and she came to our house. She
said to my mam, 'you have a nice home.' Mam was offended, she said, 'oh, you
expect us to be dirty do you?' She probably shouldn't have said that. But mam
had 12 children to bring up and no money but her house was always spotless.
One of her sons ended up in the Foreign Office, did really well, another was a
dustman, and all in between!

My mam said I couldn't keep the baby. I was put in a home on Elswick Road
for unmarried girls. I lived in anguish all those months, waiting my turn to have
my baby taken away. I wanted to keep it. I saw other girls have theirs taken from
them. It was like waiting to be shot. I had the baby and she was beautiful. My
younger sister was clever, and she persuaded mam to come and see me and the
baby, she said you're not human if you don't go. So mam came up and she was
nursing the baby the whole time she was there. She looked at me and said, 'would
you like to keep her?' After all the anguish and worry I'd been through! Mam
said you can bring her home, she's beautiful! We went to court to fight for
maintenance. Her dad lied, said he wasn't working but he was. They said he'd

have to pay 15 shillings a week until she was 16. He only paid for 6 months then stopped. The police went to take him back to court but then I got a letter from his mam in Scotland. I kept all her letters until I was married and my husband made me destroy them. She offered to take over paying for my daughter's keep, I sent her photographs and I think she could see her son in her, but she never met the bairn, and I never met her, though I kept writing to her for years. Her letters stopped when the bairn was 15, I think she must have passed away, then another relative offered to pay but I told them to stop. They'd been so kind. Her dad, well I never saw him again and he never tried to see his daughter. She was fair, very fair, and blue eyed like him. Well it was only a one night stand. Later on she said, 'I'm going to Scotland to find my father!' And her husband said, you're married to me now, you don't need him.

When my daughter was four years of age, I got married. I had 7 more children with my husband! He was violent to me, but how could I leave my children? I had nowhere to go and couldn't take them with me. We stayed in the marriage for 30 years. At first, he was the only feller I met who didn't want me for sex, but for me. Not easy, when I had a child already, to meet men. He was willing to wait until we married to have sex. But then he got me pregnant time after time, eight times (I lost one). I tried everything for birth control but I couldn't control him. He did it on purpose. But my children were a blessing. He was seven years older than me and a very jealous man. I met him at a wedding, I took one look and said I'm not going out with him! But I married him. Thirty years through all the troubles. He'd just come out the army, and he didn't tell me til years later but he'd got wounded in the head. He got a low wage job in the gas board. I worked til I was pregnant, but we had no home, little money, we lived with his mam in their flat. She didn't want us there, but I couldn't live with my mam, we fought for years!

My mother had a welfare social worker, Miss F, who visited us and admired my mother for how she kept the house and brought up all her twelve children. This woman had lots of little girls named after her in the area. Me mother worked for her in her posh house in Brighton Grove, cleaning and that. I used to help with the cleaning when me mam had trouble bending and so on. When Miss F died, my mam was left some money by her, we had to go to a solicitor. Me mam gave me and me sister gifts of money. She gave me enough for a deposit on a house. We bought a flat from a lovely Jewish guy who lived in Gateshead. But we had no money to keep it up. We heard that if you gave up your house or flat to the council, you'd get a council house. We did, and we got a house in Blakelaw. Now I live in a lovely sheltered flat of my own.

My husband wouldn't work. He'd take on jobs and then not turn up or stop going. He told me he was learning to be a driver, but he was learning to be a drinker. He went to the club down the road, he was in the pub every night. I was expecting our second child (by him, my third) by then. He was a very jealous man and didn't let me go anywhere. He kept getting me pregnant, whatever I did. It turned out it was to get the maternity benefit lump sums! He became violent and beat me up often. I nagged him about working as we had no money and all these eight children coming one after another, and then he'd attack me. I had seven babies in 9 years, and a miscarriage. I never enjoyed sex. When I was five months pregnant with my 8th child, I couldn't take it any more and took an overdose. We were both saved, and my youngest daughter turned out to be a blessing to me. And her daughter cares for me now!

When my daughter was born I was in Princess Mary Hospital, and the doctor said, 'what's the matter with you?' I said, 'I'll take me life rather than have any more babies.' Five days after she was born, I had me tubes tied. But I'd torn my bladder during my last childbirth. It didn't get repaired for ten years! They all said it was in my mind, they wouldn't even look. This one woman doctor, I still remember her, she said 'there's nothing wrong with you.' I suffered, and I couldn't sleep. With all those children to bring up and working all day as well. When they eventually found out about the bladder tear, I had a big operation to repair it.

Well my husband was violent to me for years. He was even worse when he didn't drink! I didn't tell a soul. The children didn't know at first, he only did it when they were in bed. He never laid a finger on them, and believe it or not, they loved him, he was a good father in how he treated them, though he was violent to me, and we were so poor because he wouldn't work. Then this one time, he threw me across the floor, knocked a tooth out, and tried to strangle me, there were marks on my neck for all to see. I had to go to hospital. I told the Doctor, and he called my husband in and gave him a talking to. My husband came home with his head hanging, and told me the doctor said, 'if you hit her once more, I'm going to see to it you go to prison for 6 months.' After that he stopped doing it. A few times he started to, but I'd remind him. And once later, our son heard him and came downstairs, and said to him, 'I'll bloody kill you if you hit my mam.' When my youngest was 2, I gave up nagging my husband to work, and I went out to work instead, scrubbing floors, cleaning, anything to get some money. He looked after the kids, he was good with them! He died a terrible death, in 1983. Cancer of the gullet. He wouldn't tell anyone at first until it was too late. When he was dying, I'd ask him, do you love me? He'd say, I've always loved you. But a couple of days before he died, I went towards him but he made shooing movements with his hands as if to push me away. So I think he didn't love me. I became a Christian and I forgave him for everything he did.

After he died, I met a man. He was impotent, he told me. I told him, so am I. But I loved him, and he loved me. We met through Church, we were both Christians. He treated me well and took me on holidays. He died of leukaemia. When I dream, he's the one I dream about.

PEGGY, 81

A lifetime of caring, despite sexual abuse in childhood and anti-German prejudice during wartime.

I want to tell you about a hard childhood and a hard life. My grandpa was German, he had a bakery, and my mam and dad worked in the bakery. When I was nine, they give me a key to let myself in after school, mam used to leave a banana and a tin of carnation milk out for me. Father worked nightshift sometimes and slept in the afternoons. My parents were very strict. I was an only child. I'm going to tell you something I've never told a soul since it happened, not even my sons. When I was about 6, my grandfather sexually assaulted me. He said he loved me, and if I loved him… so I associated love with sex from a very early age. It only happened the once, I told me mam and it stopped. I can't remember what she said to me, and I don't know what she said to him but it didn't happen again. He didn't penetrate me, he took my knickers off and rubbed against me. I'm 81, but it keeps coming back to me. I feel guilty, that I let him. And angry, yes. But I loved him! So after I told my mother, he never did it again. But yes he still lived with us, I mean it was his business they worked in so we had no choice. Yes, it does make me feel better now I've told you. Well his wife had left him when my father was a child, my grandfather brought him up. No, I don't know if he ever did anything like that to my father.

Anyway, it was coming up to the Second World War, and because he was German, he was beaten up within an inch of his life, an auntie told me later. At the time I didn't know about it, or where he was, I never visited him, he just disappeared, he was in hospital a long time it seems.

(AUTHOR'S NOTE: it occurred to me later that during this 'disappeared' time he might have been in prison, or even a mental institution getting 'treatment' as a result of the abuse. Perhaps her mother did do something more than speak to him? But this is what Peggy was told. And of course people with the wrong names and accents did get beaten up at that time, as follows in Peggy's story.)

It was terrible, people stopped coming to the bakery. My last name was German. I was bullied, boys would throw stones at me after school. The bakery had to be sold, we moved to Hull. I was ten when war broke out. We changed our name unofficially. Our ration books and the school register were in our real names, but my parents spoke to the teachers, and they agreed to use my English name. And you know, I've never told anyone my real maiden name. I still tell nobody! I just told one person who came from Bavaria like my grandfather, who came from there when he was 17 on his way to an uncle in America, only he ran out of money. He studied bakery and met my grandmother and stayed here. The person I told, tried to research my family over there but she said all the records were lost in the war. So anyway, we were in Hull, but we got bombed out and came back to Newcastle. When I was 13, my mam took ill, she was in hospital nine months, they said it was a burst ulcer, but it turned out to be cancer, she died when I was 14. After that, I had to work all day and look after my father and grandfather, both of them, oh it was hard. I was a shop assistant at the co-op.

Well I'd known my husband since I was 14, we got married on my 19th birthday, and my husband moved in with us. I had two sons. My grandfather lived to 81, he died before my sons were born, my father had health problems, I'd had to nurse them both, look after all of them, bring up my boys. By the time my father died, my boys were 12 and 14. For the first time, me and my husband and our children were on our own. Things were easier then. I loved the old men but it was hard work. Well I didn't mind, my father and grandfather came together, they were always together, because my grandfather had brought him up. In the First World War, my grandfather was interned as an enemy alien, while his son, my father, was sent to fight the Germans! But he had a German name, so they wouldn't give him a gun. They made him a stretcher-bearer instead. So anyway, when my elder son was 14, one day I went out, and my father collapsed and died in my son's arms. He's never forgotten it. My husband's been dead ten years. He'd just come out of hospital after a heart operation, we slept in twin beds because I had an orthopaedic one, next morning, I found him dead in bed. We were married in 1948, we had our golden wedding do in 1998.

I like coming here, (*a day centre*) next week I'm playing the keyboards!

AUTHOR'S NOTE: we talked about her sexual abuse revelation, about her feeling of guilt despite the fact she was six at the time and would do what grown-ups told her, and was emotionally blackmailed into it. She seemed to struggle with the fact that she did love her grandfather, and kept having to live with him and nurse him until he died. And she needed to know that he loved her, despite what he did. Also I wonder if the 'shame' of being German at that time somehow got combined with this. She said people still talked about 'Germans' in a nasty way so she still keeps her real name secret, even after all this time. On a later visit to give her a copy of the piece, she told me she felt much better for telling me about her past, and now sleeps much better.

BRENDA, 77

After years caring for an abusive husband, who was violent to their sons,
she speaks about dating happily after 70.

Brenda is neat and petite, fair, well dressed and looks a lot younger than her
years. I said so and she replied, 'it's because I've got a wig on! My hair went
thin after my hysterectomy, which I had at 37, and I've worn wigs for years.'
But in fact her face is young too.

BRENDA'S STORY:

I live in a sheltered two bedroom flat. I moved here because my husband had a
stroke and I nursed him for twelve years. He died about 8-9 years ago and I still
live here. I go to a day centre weekly. I'm very busy, I have four sons, three of
them with diabetes since childhood, who I see a lot. One of them lives down the
road and comes here every day for his dinner! I have a man friend, yes like a
boyfriend, who takes me out and about and drives me to get shopping in. I do
lots of crafts – I make cards, 'faberge' eggs, I sew, make stuffed toys, all kinds.
I'm addicted to crossword puzzles.

I've been seeing my boyfriend for about six years now. His wife died of
cancer. We go to a social club twice a week. We tried dancing but he's got two
left feet! We go out into the countryside, outings up to Hexham. After nursing
my husband for twelve years, I felt more like a nurse than a wife, but there's an
emptiness when they go. No, I wouldn't live with my boyfriend or marry again,
I like my independence! He's got a tiny miner's bungalow, he used to be a miner.
We go on holiday together. My sons all like him. Sometimes I wish I had some
peace!! He's four years younger than me. I met him through a friend. I don't
have very many friends but I have one friend who's 92, we go all over the place
on buses.

I'd not been with a man for twelve years because of my husband's stroke.
I didn't really have a happy marriage. We got on, but he was unkind and cruel to
our children, abusive, and we argued about that all the time. He thought of his
sons as rivals. He constantly hit them and criticised them especially our eldest.
When he was a child, he felt nobody loved him, his mother put his brother first

and mollycoddled him (he had a heart murmur) and ignored my husband. He often called our eldest by his brother's name! When they weren't around, it was like courting again. I kept having sons hoping for a daughter. But I had the hysterectomy. He picked on the eldest all the time, he constantly hit him on the head, and the boy developed epilepsy as well as diabetes. I always wonder if it was the hitting that caused it. One day my son started choking on some food, and my husband said to him, 'choke, you bugger, choke.' He grew up with no confidence. Why didn't I leave? Oh, I did. I went back to my mother when I had three sons. My husband kept coming round promising all sorts, begging me to come back. Then he went to my father and my father came home and ordered me to go back to him. My mother said, 'I'll go as well', but he just said, 'go ahead'. So I had no choice. In those days there was nowhere else for a woman to go. He was a good worker and provider though. My sons got diabetes when they were 8, 11, and 13 and I had to give them a lot of attention. When he had his stroke, there were two sons still at home. He was a nicer man after the stroke! He told me he loved me every single day. But he never was nice to the boys, and he never said he wished he'd been different. My eldest says to me, 'I wish my dad had talked to me.' We could have had a good marriage if he'd been kind to the children. Nursing him was my duty. Last couple of years he was in a wheelchair, it was hard.

But I have a good life now with my sons, friends and my boyfriend, my flat, my activities.

EDIE, 79
Single and alone but still feisty, after an abusive orphanage and traumatic attacks by a family member. (AC Centre)

Edie has very, very long nails with coloured varnish on them. She wears a dashing hat. She trembles all the time, and has a heavy handbag filled with treasures. She has trouble looking after herself apparently. She has small pale eyes and a bowed posture and walks with a frame.

EDIE'S STORY:

I'm 80 next week – I'm a single lady, I've never married, I don't like men, and I don't like children, and I don't like nuns! So I only like women, who aren't nuns that is! Why don't I like nuns? Well I was an orphan and I ended up in a convent orphanage. Those nuns used to hit us with anything they could get their hands on, hairbrush, ruler, anything. Not one of them was kind to us, even now I shiver when I see a nun. I lost my mother when I was five, and my father died when I was seven, killed by a lorry. I never did know what my mother died of. I had four brothers, but I never saw them again after my father died. And I had a sister who I did get to know afterwards. I belong Newcastle, I was born a stone's throw from the river Tyne. When I was orphaned, I was sent to Barnardo's, they were kind. But then when I was 12 or 13 I was sent to the nuns. After I left the convent I worked as a cleaner at Princess Mary's Maternity Hospital in Gosforth, and at a School for boys, even though I don't like children. I lived with an aunt after the convent for a while, after that I've always lived alone. Children are noisy, too noisy for me. And why I don't like men? I went to stay with my sister after I left the convent, for a holiday, and her husband wouldn't leave me alone – you know, sex. Every day. Did he rape me, I think he did. I never told my sister, she might not have taken my part, she might have taken his. I didn't know so I said nothing. All the years I knew my sister, she didn't know. So I live alone, with carers coming in. I like pleasing myself, watching TV. I've never travelled, but I like Australian soaps. I've got the shakes and feel like I'm going to fall, so I use a walker.

CHAPTER SEVEN
WORK AND WAR: MORE LIVING HISTORY

Many of the older people lived through World War Two or were directly or indirectly affected by it, or even World War One, perhaps in injury to a family member. Many were evacuated as children. War time experience, with its traumas and excitements, is a big gulf between them and those of us born after. Hard enough to live through nightly air raids, war service, evacuation, but worse, at the time, they didn't know for sure that 'our side' would win! Work lives too are varied, for both men and women. The idea that 'women didn't work' in the old days is just plain wrong. Women always worked, more educated ones until they married and were compelled to stop, and working class women throughout their lives, it just wasn't recorded or noticed, like so many aspects of ordinary people's existence. Both sexes worked hard, and long hours; leisure was snatched in the odd hour, and holidays were a day at the seaside if you could afford the train fare.

There are many tales of war and work to be found in other sections of this book of course, but in those cases, some other aspect of the story has decided its inclusion in a different area (see James Tod's story also for his flying boat war service).

JOY, 88
Knitting for public art projects, after the army and a life of other peoples' crime as a court usher. (AC Centre)

I like to do crafts. I made a clippie mat recently. I've got that at home. I go to two clubs, this one and one where we do crafts. I like to knit. Here, look at this!

I'm knitting part of a bench! It's an art project for Shipley Art Gallery. Look! (AUTHOR'S NOTE: Joy shows me a knitting pattern for a life-size park bench, an artist, Trevor Pitt, devised it and has done it elsewhere. Now it's being done here, for exhibition in Newcastle and Gateshead. Older people have been knitting a boat, a washing line of washing, etc as works of community art.)

I'm 88, 89 in October. I live alone in a flat with a warden to keep an eye on all of us, but we look after ourselves. I see my daughter who lives here and go to visit my other daughters down south and in Glasgow. I have heart trouble but I like to get involved in things and get to know people.

I used to work at Newcastle Crown Court, as an Usher, when I was young, about 20. I used to wear a black gown. I had to look after the jury and make sure they didn't go out or speak to anybody about the case. I had to swear in the witnesses. Oh yes, I heard some grisly cases, some of the evidence was horrible, murders, all sorts, but you had to take it in your stride. I had to organise the judge's papers, they were all in a file with pictures of bodies and suchlike. I loved that job. Some of the barristers were so clever, it was a privilege to hear them speak. You'd make your mind up somebody was guilty, then they'd speak and you could see it all a different way.

Then I got called up during the war, into the army, the ATS. My poor mother was in tears, but I enjoyed it. I spent the war in Scotland and the South, posted to Leicester for three years. I was a Corporal by the end. I got married while I was in the army, he was in the navy. We looked forward to the war ending and having a happy married life and a home and children. But it didn't work out quite like that. We were too different I suppose. We got demobbed and lived together and had three children, three girls. As they got older, I really thought...I wasn't happy. He was very bossy and 'knew everything'. I'd got my confidence in the army! We did split up but we didn't get divorced. He started working away and I didn't mind. Well I went out with one or two men but nothing serious. I had three children to bring up. They were my life. They've all done well.

Look at this. My daughter sent me this. That photograph on the front, is me as a child, my mother and my mother's mother!

NOTE: Joy gets out a National Theatre programme, with a photograph illustrating their recent production of a 1947 play 'Men Should Weep'.

I discovered that Joy's daughter, credited for the photo, is founder of a TV company, and a Bafta winning film maker. The photo is attributed online as taken in 1933.

GWEN, 88 AND AUDREY, 85

Friends enjoying crafts together, from different backgrounds, talk about their lives and war service adventures in the Land Army and the Wrens.
(AC Centre)

At an Age Concern Day Centre, they were all doing some jewellery making, and a lady was going round giving them aromatherapy massages while they worked and talked.

GWEN'S STORY: POSTING A RABBIT STOLEN FROM A STOAT, AS A HUNGRY LANDGIRL!

I'm 88. I live in a sheltered bedsit. I've been there 24 years now. I have a carer who comes in daily. I use a wheelchair as I've got Meniere's disease.

I left school when I was fourteen and went to work in a greengrocer's. But then the war started, so while I was waiting to be called up, I worked on the United buses, going to Carlisle and Hexham, taking the fares. Then my call up papers came. I was in the Land Army, in the Timber Corps. We chopped down big trees with axes and sawed them up for pit props, and the hard wood went for furniture. It was hard work but all outdoors, and I loved every minute of it. You could smell the resin in the tree trunks. Lovely. I was 21. I asked to be sent near home as my mam was a widow, but they sent me to Devon and Cornwall! Beautiful there though.

One day in the woods, I saw a stoat kill a rabbit! Well I took the rabbit away from the stoat, I gutted it, and on my way home I stopped at the post office and posted the dead rabbit to my mother – she was thrilled! It was a lovely plump rabbit. No, I didn't wrap it up, I just tied a label on it and sent it bare! Oh yes you could do that in those days. And the post was much faster, it would still be fresh when she got it.

My mum was left a widow at 35. I sent her 2/6 a week out of my pay. We wore dungarees, and for dress uniform, jodhpurs, a green sweater and a green beret. I got a medal and a letter from the prime minister, just this year or last year, I was pleased to get it! We lived in a camp. We got beetroot sandwiches for wor bait, sometimes with cheese in.

My father was only 40 when he died, and my brother died only ten days later, he was 8 years old. Well my father was in the trenches in the First World War, he was bitten by a rat and he had good healing flesh and it healed over. But then when he was forty, he had all his teeth out and it turned out to be gangrene and it killed him. They told me it was the rat.

(AUTHOR'S NOTE: perhaps more likely to be the dentist's unsterile instruments?)

They said my brother died of a broken heart, because he hadn't cried. He wasn't ill, I just came home one day and he was dead. Me and my sister lived on, my sister died a few years ago. Times were hard for us with my father dead but I had a lovely childhood and wonderful parents. My mam got 10/- a week pension. After the war, I got a job in the NAAFI bar. I met my husband there. He'd be in the bar when we opened, until we shut. I didn't catch on, it was because of me! We married in 1948, we had very happy years together. He died of coronary thrombosis. We had one son, who's 60 now. He lives down south. I've been a widow a long time, but I wouldn't marry again. I could never put anybody in my Jock's place. When he died I had a row with the woman who said I'd not get his pension, I wrote a six page letter and I did get it in the end!
Oh I'm quite happy. I've had a good life.

AUDREY'S STORY: DANCING, MARCHING AND FLYING THE FLAG.

I'm 85, I live in the same sheltered bedsits as Gwen. I walk with a walker, not very much though. I've had hip and knee replacements and arthritis. I grew up in Whitley Bay, I was an only child and sent to a small private school in Marine Avenue, 'Norwood', where I left at 16. I took 'matric', matriculation, the way you qualified then, but I didn't go to university. They told me I'd have to teach afterwards and I didn't want to. So I took a commercial course instead, secretarial, and got a job in a solicitor's office in North Shields. It was very formal, we all used second names at all times. I enjoyed the job, I got £1 a week and gave my mother half. After a year, someone else came and forced a raise for us to 35/- a week. I went to dances at the Empress, and later in town, at the Oxford and the Assembly Rooms.

During the war, I joined the WRNS, I was 18. I was put in the Signals Distribution office, I took phone calls and forwarded them to the right people. We worked shifts of 8 hours. I was stationed at Leith, Edinburgh. I was lucky, it was beautiful. On night duty, we had to haul down the Union Jack flag and at dawn, we had to haul it up again. One time I hauled it up upside down! All the ships rang in asking what was going on! I was in the victory procession on Princes Street, we couldn't walk in step because there were three bands playing in competition! And I remember being in the street on VE day, the word was being passed round, and everyone was hugging each other. After the war, I worked in an accountant's office. I met my husband in a rambling club we both belonged to. We had two sons, one of them got into Cambridge to do maths. He's not interested in people. He lives there on his own, never married and hasn't been to see me for ten years. He always sends Marks and Spencers tokens and cards for Christmas and my birthday though. My other son never married either, he lives nearby and I see him a lot. I married in 1951, and my husband died in 1994 of lung cancer, though he never smoked. But he worked in a drawing office, where everybody smoked all the time. I had my husband 43 years, I've had a happy life though I'd have liked to have my husband with me for longer.

AUTHOR'S NOTE: it's interesting to observe how age seems to minimise the divisions between people imposed by social class, affluence and education.

MARJORIE, 80

Wartime evacuation, hard work, marriage and widowhood. (DCP)

I was evacuated in the war. To Crook, near Kendal. We'd to help on the farm, hay making, corn, potato picking. We used to jump off the hay loft, there was a hay fork in the hay and I jumped and it went through my leg! Probably still got a hole in my leg. They just put a bandage on it. There was a field behind the farmhouse, with a stone 'monument' we called it, on a steep hill beside a pond we used to skate on. Our names are carved on the monument, still there! We went recently, my brother climbed up to look. Three of us went, me, my brother and younger sister. I was ten, he was nine, she was seven. My other two sisters weren't thought of then. Mam used to come and visit, Dad was sent to London to mend damaged gas pipes in the blitz. We were upset being parted from Mam. First place I went, was a couple on their own, they were very good to me. We were separated, then the other farm, where my brother and sister were, sent for me to join them. They had a son in the RAF and two in the ATS. Mam sent us a Christmas parcel, but they gave it to their daughter, we had to watch her playing with our toys while we got nowt, Mam had written and told us what we'd be getting. I wrote to Mam and she took us back. She said something to them when she came to take us home, that was in 1942. I don't know what it was. She'd paid for we, as well!

Then I went to Westgate Hill School, left when I was 14. I'll never forget Mr Partridge, a teacher, who strapped me. It (*the mark left by the leather strap*) was right up my arm! My Mam went up to them, mind, when she saw it. I didn't do anything, the lad behind me flicked paper and hit the teacher, he thought it was me. I worked at a dressmaker's, didn't like it, then the YMCA, then at Mackays, we called it 'Mackies', till I was 32, when I got married, and had four children. I worked at a school for blind children, I loved that job, for twenty odd years. I was just a cleaner, but we got roped in for all sorts. I kept a little lad company one day, blind and deaf, he was waiting for somebody, and he said he wished he had his hearing, but he didn't mind being blind.

I met my husband at my sister's wedding. She was talking to him when I went to talk to her, and it was her new husband's brother! We were married three months after her! We were sure. I'd had a few before you know, but it was just like that, we clicked straight away. Love at first sight. I think that can happen. No, nobody said we were rushing things, my father knew him and his family you see. He came from Scotswood, and I came from Big Lamp. He was an overhead linesman, electric and that, pylons. Well one day he came in from a darts match, sat down, and asked for a cup of tea. I went to make it and brought it in to him, I said here's the tea you asked for, I shook him – he'd had a massive heart attack. He was 54. We'd been married 18 years. He'd had a numb left arm, chest pains. The doctor took too long to come out, I think they could've saved him. It took two hours. He was still warm, that's how I know. The police came, they took away his medicine the doctor'd given him for heartburn. They said it was alright. They got in touch with my sister and my Mam, they came straight down. Mam stayed a fortnight. Somebody came, don't know who it was, offered to take the bairns off me for a while, I said, 'nobody takes my bairns! I'll manage.' My daughter was in the house at the time, she was eleven. She got sent to my sister's in a taxi. While she was there, she got her uncle to pay for her to get her ears pierced, though her dad had said no, she was too young! After her dad died, she started playing truant, I think it was the trauma.

I've got two sons still living with me, one's been married and divorced, the other never married. They run after me, they won't let me do anything in the house! One son is married with three step children, he lives in my street. My daughter married at 16, had four children, all girls. She calmed down after that for a while. But I was rushed to hospital, I think it was pneumonia, I was in a coma. After that I lived with her for 18 months. Then one day, she took me out to tea at some folks', I didn't know them, then she took me back to my house and said, 'you're here for good now!' I only had the clothes I stood up in. She said I could fetch the rest. She was going to get divorced and live with somebody else, that's why she put me out then.

How do I feel about being older? I'm 80. Well I sit and knit, and crochet. Coming here's done me good, I've made friends, I come two days a week. I like to sit on the balcony and smoke! The worst thing about being old? You feel helpless. But I'm quite happy.

BILLY, 83

Running a family haulage and farming business and important national disaster management: a lifetime of hard, but enjoyable work vividly remembered.
(AL SOC Centre)

I'm from Newburn. We have our own family business, haulage, road transport. Like Eddie Stobart? No, he was like us! My father started it and I followed him into it. He started with a horse and flat cart, built it up from there until we had forty-odd lorries, and three farms! I was educated at Throckley School. I'd be at school all day, go home, have my tea, then I'd be down to the office to work for my father, I had to do my homework there while I was waiting for the drivers to come in from all over, I worked until late. We lived in an end terraced house, later it became the police house. My father had a big advertisement painted on the gable end, there was a big crossroads just there and everyone could see it. My father also set his brother up in business. Our three farms were at Throckley, then one near Ponteland, and one out west. In summer, we all had to go and work there, bringing in the hay, after a full day's school or work, we'd work until ten at night on the farms. My father worked very hard, he'd be up at six and he'd not get home until nine at night. That's haulage, you have to be there. If it's your own business, you don't have time to be off, you have to start when all the workers start, and finish after them. I have one sister, she went to college and became a cook, she ended up teaching it. Mother looked after the family, she had to do a lot of cooking, we were hungry and worked long hours, and father would often bring some of the drivers back to eat with us, so she always had to make extra food! If it wasn't needed, she'd pass it on down the street to people less well off.

Then in the war I became a Bevan Boy, I was sent to work down the pit, the Maria pit, for two years. Well I had the business to go into, but I came from a mining village and knew lots of lads down the pit. But about that time, my father had a serious illness, and I kept taking time off the mine to keep the business going, and they got fed up and took me out the pit, and said I'd have to go in the Army instead! It was the end of the war and I wanted to go to work but had to do another two years national service in the army. I could have got out of it, but my father didn't want people to think that his son took advantage. When I started in the business, father made me start at the bottom and do all the worst jobs. If you do that, nobody can come back and say you just got made manager. I drove long distance lorries all over, with our best driver, he was like family. (NOTE: This driver was the father in law of the staff member who was with us and had lived in same area as Billy, and knew the business well.)

I ended up as manager, with lorries up to 20 tons. I enjoyed haulage. You have to be always thinking, how to get the most business, how to maximise the loads, how to get the most use of the lorries. You have to keep materials moving all the time, that's where others go wrong. Haulage is a competition, it's good to have something challenging. My father would say, 'there's 24 hours in a day, and nobody stops you working!' My father was very strict, and he'd made it his business. But then I wanted to do something of my own, and have my own honour, if you know what I mean. He'd only use his ideas, and sometimes mine were better. And I also wanted to find out how other people worked, if they had good new ideas we could use, so I left the business and started working for British Road Services, working for the Ministry.

I got to the top, I was put in charge of all the 'crash' jobs – disasters and big events. There was a big east coast flood, I was made the controller of all the work to put it right. They held back the Flying Scotsman at Newcastle Central Station for fifteen minutes just for me, the police escorted me onto the train. I went south to take control, I was there maybe six months. I had to organise lorries from all over, to bring stone to build up the defences where the north sea was breaking through and flooding. You have to organise the fleet to get materials in, but there's more to it, you have to make sure there's fuel for the lorries and food for the drivers, you have to set up canteens, all sorts. Oh, I didn't get paid any extra, just my usual monthly amount! But I enjoyed it, and at the end, you can stand back and say, I did that! I was also responsible for organising the Queen's visit to the Town Moor, for the special exhibition. It took nine months to organise. She shook my hand! Probably in the 1970's? My wife didn't meet the Queen, no. No, I don't think she was jealous. She'd not like to hear that – my wife was from a very different background! She came from Hartlepool, we met in the army, we were both in the Pay Corps, travelling around organising all the army pay. We had two children, one of each. My son went into the business. My daughter lives next door to me and my wife now! It's an open shop! Both my children went to a good school. My father used to say, they can take anything away from you, but they can't take a good education. He'd hammer that into me. He thought I should be working for him, instead of the ministry. Yes he was probably proud of me, but he'd never have said it!

Oh well I didn't have hobbies or anything as I worked such long hours. I still work in the haulage business, helping out. I still like working out how to get the best out of the business. I have grandchildren, but young people now don't seem as keen to get on with business, they'd not work hours after school every day these days!

If I had any advice for young people, I'd say, decide what you want to do, and what you want to be, aim for that, and you'll get it in the end. Don't worry if you haven't got the money, look about you and you'll find it. Go to the bank and have all your information available. The banks are the most honest people. I'm 83 now. I've had a good life.

AUTHOR'S NOTE: Billy was articulate and intelligent and very keen on his haulage business and work life. But afterwards I learned that the business had closed about 30 years ago. He was very fluent and his memory was amazing, he couldn't remember any dates though and if he tried to think of one he'd realise something wasn't right and he'd say 'I don't know what's wrong with me today, you've caught me on a bad day I think.' He was very cheerful otherwise. Very smart too. He's partly deaf but could hear if I spoke up, he's got one hearing aid and is getting another.

The floods of 1953, in Essex, were the worst peacetime natural disaster ever in the UK, with 300 dead in the UK, and thousands in Holland.

SALLY

Working in wartime. (AL SOC Centre)

Sally presented as very quiet and hesitant, seeming to have trouble organising her sentences, though using articulate language. Clearly she'd had a responsible job and had been very much under pressure not to make mistakes, this weighs on her mind even now. I felt she was going round and round a story which she either forgot or can't bring herself to tell. Something about money she was responsible for, maybe a halfpenny fell on the floor ... she talked about air raids and rushing out, maybe money got taken when she left it on the desk? Or maybe it was so drummed into her she'd be blamed, that's why it keeps on going through her mind.

SALLY'S STORY.

I worked ten years in Littlewoods Store opposite Fenwicks. The people who worked there were really well noticed, there was a lovely atmosphere with the staff. When I get on the bus, there'll be somebody who says, 'oh, it's Sally!' Funny things went on in Littlewoods. I was in charge of the office, there was a good side and a bad side, I was in charge of the money and paying the wages out. The war was on. People used to have to run into the air raid shelters. We all carried our gas masks at all times. Money had to be exactly right or they'd know! The money was all in big bags. Cotton bags. You could tie the top. There was a store detective. When you added your money up, it had to be dead on. If there was a halfpenny missing it had to be reported to the manager. The store detective used to stand at the top of the escalator and say, 'open your bag!' You had to open your bag. You had your own typewriter, to put the money in the accounts, if it didn't add up... my husband was going mad, this went on for quite a while, because I was on this side of the store. When I was on the cash, you had to be careful what you were doing. There was a woman wouldn't leave the shop, thought she'd been short changed.

My daughter gave birth to twins last night. One of each. I've not seen them yet, she hasn't chosen names yet. Beautiful. Two lovely twins!

NOTE: She told me this several times. I couldn't tell if it's a grand-daughter recently had twins, or her daughter decades ago.

SYLVIA

Product of a wartime romance, is still bilingual despite dementia, and loves to dance. (DCP Centre)

She was with her two sons. She spoke to me in French and was very pleased when I answered her in French. Very feisty woman! Her sons were very loving, very open about using the word dementia. She didn't argue with it but she did give firm opinions about everything else.

SYLVIA'S STORY: My mother was French. I don't like being old. I always used to go to dancing, I don't dance much now. I miss it. As long as I've got company though! People who like doing what I like. As long as I'm with my sons, I'm happy. I like it here, and where I've been staying. You get to know people. I go back over my life and I've not done badly. My mother, father and me lived in Peebles, Scotland. My father played piano in a cinema for the silent films, and I got in for nothing! My friend's father owned the cinema. So I had a happy childhood. My mother was French and I still speak French. My father went over there in the First World War, met a French girl, and they got married, had two sons and two daughters. His mother wasn't happy he married a French girl!

NOTE: Sylvia, as well as speaking French, kept bursting into song, she sang the Marseillaise. She enjoyed dancing and singing at the centre. Her sons were concerned she was needing more help but not yet a care home. An awkward transition for many older people especially those with dementia.

HARRY, WILLEM, AND DEREK

Wartime and work tales. (DCP Centre)

HARRY was a very articulate man, with very detailed memories and knowledge, he kept telling us (a group all gathered round talking at the Day Centre) he was going into hospital next week and we'd not see him for eight weeks, everyone went along with this but apparently it's not so, or not any longer. Otherwise he showed no obvious signs of dementia.

HARRY'S STORY: I'm nearly 81. I worked for Post Office Telephones (*now BT),* I was in charge of installing the systems at Eldon Square and at Durham University. Durham was difficult, Durham Cathedral, too, all very old walls, you had to get special permission to drill holes in for the wires! And the Nissan factory in Sunderland, that was a huge job.

Well I was evacuated during the war, lost some schooling. I didn't stay away long. I was sent to Staffield Hall, a big place with dormitories. Mam wanted me home. She was a nurse at the General Hospital, and she was head air raid warden. We all carried gas masks. We heard the Germans had invented a new gas, so all the gas masks were changed, you had to put tapes on them, I did that for Mam. She was in charge of the shelter on Atkins Road, underneath the Library. She let me blow the whistle! She took me to Tiverton in Devon, but the train stopped on the way because of the Coventry Air Raid, biggest of the war. I saw and heard Coventry burning. The train moved on come daylight.

I was 14 in 1944 so I was too young to be in the forces, but I've spent my life as a Sergeant in the Territorial Army. I've been to Germany twice, Wales, all over with them.

My dad came back from Dunkirk, after the Germans captured it. He came home wearing a Navy uniform, the captain of the ship he was on made him wear it because his army uniform was all oily. The navy charged him for the uniform! He said, no wonder a captain goes down with his ship!

My dad came home from the war, and employed me in his shoe business, but on condition that I did J1 and J2 at nightschool. Then I became a bus conductor! One day, on the bus to Gateshead, the bus was very crowded, I was upstairs getting all the fares, somebody got on downstairs and hadn't bought a ticket. Somebody reported it to the bus company, and I had to go to Head Office to explain myself! So I said to them, I want me cards! I left, and outside the Oxford was a labour exchange, I went in and asked for a job. I said I'm 21 tomorrow. They said, here's a green card, take this, go down here and ask for a job. It was for a private phone company. So I did. And later, I worked for Post Office Telephones, first as an engineer, in Inverness, then I went to Bletchley for a month's course, and got promoted to Manager. I ended up supervising all those major installations, Nissan, Eldon Square, etc.

I asked, did he know my father? Aye, I knew him, I was a fitter when he was manager.

I got married in the oldest church in Newcastle, do you know which that is? St Andrews! My TA regiment were there, based on Barrack Rd. The piper was waiting for us at the church. When did I get married, well me daughter's 44! She has her own antiques business, and she works part time at the Civic Centre.

What do I do now, I play tapes and records, I like war time songs, I've got Vera Lynn and Ann Shelton harmonising on one. Ann used to sing with Ambrose. Glenn Miller asked her to sing with him but Ambrose wouldn't release her. But then Glenn Miller went missing anyway. Architecture, that's me main interest, I've got a lot of books about that. Did you know Thomas Grainger, who Grainger Street's named after, he had thirteen daughters, they've all got streets named after them! And I come here and talk to my friend Willem and the other lads. But I won't be here next week, you'll not see me for 8 weeks, I'm going into hospital for an operation.

WILLEM sat next to Harry, they were good friends, sometimes they gave the impression they'd been friends for many years but actually they met through DCP.

WILLEM: I'm from Holland. I was in the Dutch Merchant Navy. I was on the Vollendam, a big troop ship, for 2 thousand troops. I've been all over the world. I got bombed on board ship, we had to abandon ship. The ship was sent to Liverpool for repair, I was sent to Newcastle and put on another ship, for the same company, a passenger ship. I got married to a local girl in Newcastle, and I've been here ever since! I worked for Smiths Docks and North East Marine. I've got a youngster, a girl. I come from a place near Arnhem, ten miles from there, my parents lived near Apeldoorn, you know it?

DEREK.

Derek was very restless, repeatedly asking about how he was to get home, and who was going to give him a lift, and when were they going, and we all told him as if he'd never asked before, that it was all arranged and he was going to have his tea and cake first, he had the most obvious dementia symptoms.

DEREK: I was on submarines during the war, aye. I was a wireless operator. I was 18 when I went on them. I liked the submarines! I first went to sea on a Corvette, escorting convoys. The 'Abelia'. I went to France on D Day on the Corvette. I was sent to Blyth for training, 1941,42. The sub was called the Springer. You had lockers to keep your gear in and you sat on them!

WIN, 93

Who managed pubs with her husband, though she doesn't drink! (AC Centre)

Well I've just had an ordinary life! We managed pubs. My husband was an engineer in Egypt during the war, he had a trip to Israel and Palestine while he was there, they weren't fighting then! He brought me back a leaf from the garden of Gethsemane, I've still got it! That was 1943. Then we managed the pubs, my father had the Golden Lion on City Road, we had the Lord Nelson, then the White Horse in South Shields, then the Duke of Wellington in Newcastle, for twenty years. But I don't smoke or drink, never did! Why? Well I was a bit staid, always wanted to do the right thing. But we had the pubs, because, well, my father got us a pub to run. We had nice quiet pubs. Folk were different in those days. When we retired, my husband was 63, I was 61, it was just getting rowdy in the pubs. A young man came in, a singer, he was just nineteen, he got quite well known – anyway he got rowdy and my husband had to throw him out. It was Jimmy Nail! We had one son, he's an engineer. I'm 93 now, my husband died at 79, blind, after a stroke. A lovely man. I've a sister in Canada, she's 90. I've been out a few times, but I won't see her again now.

I've had an ordinary, good life.

STUART

A proper 'Jack the lad', a life of boozing, roaming the world, and disreputable behaviour with 'Big Ruby' from the brothel... (DCP Centre)

Stuart sits in a wheelchair, he's paralysed down one side and finds speech difficult due to this and is hard of hearing. He's thin, but has had a lot of him removed, according to a staff member and to Stuart himself! When I met him, he was watching a cowboy film and saying he didn't remember being in the battle of Little Big Horn.

When the film ended I asked him to talk to me. He was happy to.

STUART'S STORY.

I was in the forces. Army, navy, merchant navy. Then I was a city engineer for Newcastle, helped build the new Scotswood Bridge, and the roads that go over it. I've had seven strokes. One every February for seven years.

I won £286,000 on the football pools! Before the lottery came out. I was in hospital, they told me, it's nearly quarter of a million. Well I'd have spent it all in one day! So I asked them to look after it for iz. Bought shares in United Biscuits! I was a hell of a drinker. Always bliddy drunk! I had a good mother and father, mother's been dead 13 year. And I've not been in a bar for 13 year. Aye, I gave it up when me mam died. Youngest sister looks after iz now. Ah, I was Grade One in the army and in the navy, but then I had a tumour on me brain. Started having fits. It was the tumour. They cut it out. I've still got the hole! (*he points out the dent in his head*). It's like I've got little volcanoes on me brain and they erupt and I get strokes. I'm paralysed all down me left side. Whey I didn't know a stroke could kill you! They put iz in Hunters Moor hospital. I'm 10 stone now, but I was 22-26 stone for years! I was 56 inches round me waist! Aye, that was the beer! I'm 77 now, 78 in October. Yes, lucky I'm still here. I've had the last rites three times, but god hasn't wanted iz. People I knaa dying around iz, but not me. I've got four good carers, and six good nurses, and two good wardens. I live ower there.

The surgeon took most of me bowels out. And when he took some bits off iz, he says, 'you'll not get the horn no more! You're finished with women now! But just run your finger doon their noses, it's just as good as sex!' All the nurses was walking around with their hands over their noses!

I lived in Australia for four year. I was on Norwegian tankers, I got a pension from the Norwegian government. I went up to Fremantle. Wey I got drunk, and they left without iz! Left iz me passport though. So, I went straight to the brothel, and picked up 'Big Ruby', 22 stone she was. Cracked me ribs when she got hold of iz. I moved in with her, for four years. Worked on the tugboats. I think I've got a daughter! She'd be... born in 1950... I've not seen her, no. See, Big Ruby just had the baby, a little lassie, Little Ruby I think she called her, and she started asking iz for more money, well I give her £40 a month, that was a lot in the fifties! She wanted more, so I went to the harbourmaster, said I need a passage home, he says there's one coming, bound for England, they need a motorman, look after the engines. So I just left! No I didn't tell her. I got a letter from them once, Big Ruby said she was working at the brothel as a cleaner, I thought she'll be doing a bit on the side, like! And Big Ruby was from Gateshead!

I was sent to Korea when I was 17. Spent 4 months in Hiroshima, in their pox hospital. All of us got two medals, the UN medal and the Korea one. Oh aye, well after the bomb and the war. They were putting up all new buildings. I was still in the army then.

After Australia, I came home, worked for the council. Did I feel bad about Ruby? Never thought about it! Me mother was a big catholic, she'd've killed iz. I've been twice to Lourdes through her. Never been since I had me strokes though.

I've had some good times. If I had it all over again, I'd do it exactly the same! I grew up near the old Scotswood bridge, lived with me granny and me mam and dad. There was a cafe there, when I was a teenager,they had a big juke box. I started drinking very young. I'll die where I live now, I like it there, and I like it here, we make things here. I had to put the lollipops in the Christmas crackers!

Oh I was 26 stone, then 8 or 9 year ago, I stopped being big. I was in hospital after me strokes. They fed iz on cabbage water! I lost all the weight. One day they sez to iz, today you get a big dinner. It was a cabbage leaf! They said, do you want salt on that? Cheeky buggers. They took all me bowels oot. Nurses come twice a day to flush iz oot.

How did I fight in the war when I was so big? Wey, I just had to lie there with a machine gun. I was a sniper. All the UN had forces in Korea, man!

CONNIE, 81
Tells of war, marriage, divorce and dogs.
(AL SOC Centre)

I was nine when the war started. My father was in London, he went there to be an ARP warden, we worried about him, in the air raids. He was in the First World War as well. My parents married late in life. I had wonderful parents. They used to come out and play with us, other parents did as well. They'd play skippy with us.I was an only child. My father had a family already, his children were grown up, his wife had died, so I had three half sisters, and one half brother. They were lovely with me! I went to the church school, then I worked in the Co-op drapery department until I got married. They made married women leave. But later they asked me to go back. I loved my job! I met my husband through a friend. He knew her boyfriend, we went out as a four then as a couple. He was in the RAF doing national service. We married in 1950, he was a good husband. We had two children, a boy and a girl. But in fact, I'm divorced. It was when the children were grown up. I don't really know what happened, things just… seemed to go wrong. We're still friends! He still comes round. I still care for him, and he still cares for me. Why get divorced? Well he was going around with someone else at the time, and I think she wanted it. But they never married. He never married again, and neither did I. He was a good husband and a very good father. I've lived alone since, I'm quite happy. I've a lovely daughter, and granddaughter. My daughter's husband died when my granddaughter was little, so I helped to bring her up. My daughter was a nurse. It was hard for her. My granddaughter is 22 now, and married. I'm dying to be a great grandma! I don't see my son anymore. He was a good son, a very good son to me. But his wife doesn't like me. I only saw his two children when they were little. I wouldn't know them now if I saw them. And he lives just up the road. I've not seen him for a long time. My children were no bother, really!

NOTE: Connie repeated some snatches of stories many times but was accurate and fluent and never groping for a word. She kept returning to her son and grandchildren, and showed signs of tears then, otherwise was very cheerful.

Staff told me she has carers going in to her own home and has good family support. She apparently left the room when her dementia diagnosis was being announced, but she knows her doctor and likes him, and she's aware what kind of doctor he is.

CONNIE AGAIN.

I'm quite happy, I don't feel any different being older, my daughter says I'll never grow up, I'm like Peter Pan! I've loads of friends! I see my daughter and granddaughter. I've had all kind of pets, and I've always had dogs. I had King Charles Spaniels, and looked after the vicar's spaniels when he went on holiday. *(Connie was wearing a King Charles spaniel gold pendant).* My daughter has three basset hounds, I sometimes look after them.

I like knitting. I used to knit for shops to sell, baby clothes, and so on. I used to knit for Africa. Now I knit scarves for the Ukraine. My granddaughter goes there and visits a girl, she brings her back for holidays, a lovely little thing.

SARAH AND ELLEN

Hard past times for Sarah, new problems for Ellen.
(AC Centre)

Sarah and Ellen have been coming to a centre together once a week for eight years. Sarah is thin and quick and bright, though she keeps apologising, thinking she has spoken out of turn. Her hands are very much changed by arthritis. Strange elongated shapes, rather elegant actually. She has great trouble walking too. Ellen is a well made-up, smartly dressed, neatly permed lady who seems quite well off and wears many rings and jewels. We talk about wedding rings. Ellen says she has two rings, her husband bought her a new one when she couldn't get the old one on any more. He died about eight years ago. Sarah says her husband bought her a new ring when she lost the old one playing with the bairns on the beach, she wasn't bothered to get a new one but he went ahead

SARAH'S STORY.

My mother died when I was four, leaving six girls. I was the youngest. She had cancer. Dad brought us all up, even though he worked every day. He'd say, 'it's six against one, I canna win!' but we all spoilt him rotten later on. We wanted to do it, you know. Dad worked at Swan Hunters Shipyard, we went to all the launches! Dad never married again. I've a photo of my mother but only faint memories of her. Well the two eldest were only 13 and 14, and both of them had got scholarships to the grammar school, but they had to leave school and come and keep house and look after us. That was hard on them. But one of them married a footballer, he played for Hull City, so they were well off by those days' standards, though even footballers didn't earn much compared with now. I had various jobs, I was a copy typist, we had to use tippex, not like now when you can just delete! I was a shop assistant in Binns in Newcastle. I got married at 18, my husband was in the RAF, then after that he worked with electrical fitting. He died in 1990. But all my children and grandchildren went to university, and have done well. I've a son and daughter living. My daughter works for BT, in the press office, and her husband's a senior lecturer. My son and his wife are both sculptors! He did Fine Art at Newcastle University, and when he graduated with first class honours, he got a commission for a statue of St Oswald in front of the hospice. For nine months we ate, slept and breathed St Oswald, he was king of Northumbria but he visited the sick. My other son did Applied Biology at Durham University, but he was killed in an accident in his twenties. I've three grandchildren, and three great grandchildren. Some are in Canada, I've used a webcam to see them.

We were both evacuated you know! I went to Whitehaven, in Cumbria, a very kind family looked after me. I had to kiss them goodnight, we had to say 'Goodnight Daddy Craddock', that's true.'

ELLEN'S STORY:

Ellen told me her daughter has come to live near her, from York. I think, partly because, since her husband died, she's had some trouble being robbed or conned. He used to deal with all the finances. She seems well off, has been in her own bungalow for forty three years. Some roofers came and climbed on her roof and deliberately made holes, she heard them and told them to get off but was scared. She called the police. But then she had to pay somebody else to fix the holes! It cost her over £300. She is vulnerable; intelligent and articulate but too trusting. She told me she got a phone call from some nice people saying she'd won a holiday in the Cayman Islands worth thousands, she could take her daughter, only she had to pay 'taxes' to go to America... She gave them her bank details and they took £700 before her daughter found out and put a stop to it. The investigation is ongoing. Even though she knows she was scammed, she talked of some of it as if it was real. The 'taxes' for example. How good the holiday would have been. How charming they were. She seems a woman who's been loved and cherished all her life. She was evacuated to Bellingham, to a bank manager's family, he sounds rather like Mainwaring from Dad's Army. He was very kind but she didn't like him kissing her goodnight as he had a moustache!

CHAPTER EIGHT

VULNERABILITY – with the emphasis on 'ability'

Older people can be especially vulnerable to health problems, loss of friends and family, and resulting isolation. Sometimes injury or illness or the shock of bereavement robs them of autonomy or confidence. These things are not functions of old age, but more common in older people. Healing can be slow, and long stays in hospital can undermine day to day independence and even, in the case of those with dementia, identity and personal history. However, these few stories of older people up against it, either in extreme pain, in hospital away from home and family, or with advanced dementia and other conditions, even near to death, will show that their spirit and strength go on until the end, much more than is generally accepted.

INJURY: TESS

A hospital patient, terribly injured, but with her spirit intact.

Tess was very ill and injured having being hit by a car. Both legs were shattered really badly (lots of pins in both, with frames round) below the knee, shattered scapula, head injuries, punctured lung. In her eighties! A speeding driver hit her as she crossed the road in front of her house. Her mind still keen and sharp, she was desperate to get home, but in awful pain both from the injuries, the treatment, and the physio's attempts to get her up and walking. Tess and I bonded as I've had similar injuries and remember what it was like to try to stand and the agony of blood going into legs that have been 'up' for weeks. She told me a lot about her life and it's in this poem I wrote for her.

THE SOUND OF THE SEA...

... on a tape in my hospital room
Makes me think of lying in bed listening
To the sea, when it was windy in Seaton Carew.
I hear horses galloping, to the sand dunes and back,
Like they did when I was young. I would slide
Down the concrete slope, with the tide coming in,
On a cardboard box – until I sprained both ankles,
Braking too hard! And my mother put a stop to it.

We'd a shop downstairs in our front room. Tea,
Cigarettes, ham, anything on the ration. Sweets,
We'd a lot of friends at school! Mother made us pay
But I'd get my hand in the window as I went to school,
Regency bars, thick chocolate, 3 pence. A penny
A week, I got. You got 2 oz at the Toffee King,
High Street, for a farthing.

The sound of the sea makes me think
Of my work in the war,
Emptying gas meters, all pennies it was,
Weighed a ton! Gave me a double hernia,
But I still went on, I liked it, it took me
To palaces and pigsties. I can see myself now,
In my special coat (there were lots of bugs around)
Emptying meters from the Park,
To the sea front,
And the sound of the sea.

Fire watching at the gasometer, when I were sixteen,
Mother with her long hair flying, running down the road,
When she heard we'd been hit. A rumour. I'd go out

In the air raids at first, I thought it was great, mind.
Mother got under the table, sent me out for my sister!

The sound of the sea went on in the war, but
You couldn't go on the beach. All wire and concrete.
We'd go to the park instead. Where I met my husband
At a bit of a do. We had a walk round the park. I thought
He was gorgeous. Ten days we were married, then
He was in Burma. Three years. Six months of it
In hospital with dysentery, malaria. He never got over it.
I took him home. Fishing, I encouraged him to fish,
For fresh air and peace. Always home for Sunday dinner,
With green beans he grew in the garden. My Sid –
Though his real name was Cyril! I lost him at 71:
Emphysema. Last words I said to him,
'I love you sparra!' His last words to me,
'I love you.' We'd a wonderful life.

I took Tess the poem the next week, she was thrilled with it, said she'd treasure it. She'd had two more operations since last week, for MRSA, her horrific injuries gave her constant pain. This is a woman whose adored husband of ten days was sent to fight in Burma, she didn't see him for three years, ending up chronically ill with dysentery and malaria for the rest of his days, struggling to work. She lost him some years ago. They had five children, one son with chronic depression lives with her still, a granddaughter has cerebral palsy. Tess herself has had two heart bypasses, she worked in the mills from 14 years old, got a double hernia doing heavy work in the war, and now at, I think, 83 she's recovering from these appalling injuries. This lady lay there and said to me, 'I've been so lucky. I've had a wonderful life.' So typical of this generation's strength and spirit.

ADVANCED DEMENTIA

I have chosen to include the stories of older people with dementia, who are still verbally fluent, in other sections of this book. However, some of the people I've spoken to or observed have been in an advanced state of the condition and therefore have not been able to give a long interview or tell a long tale. However, I feel passionately that it is a disgrace that we still often treat those who cannot express themselves clearly in words, for whatever reason, at whatever age, as somehow being incapable of thinking, feeling, or knowing anything despite increasing evidence to the contrary. I have spent enough time with older people with dementia at all stages to be convinced that we as a society underestimate the intelligence and personality which survives, and therefore deny their humanity.

As part of this section then, I shall describe spending time with advanced dementia patients, at dementia day centres, and in hospitals.

PEARL, 94
Published writer, now disabled and with dementia, who speaks by singing.
(DCP Centre)

Pearl is 94. In the room at the Centre, amidst a group conversation going on animatedly around her, she sat very quiet, playing silent tunes to herself with her hands held as if playing a piano, and her sandaled feet tapping lightly on the floor, her sandals squeaking, all the time. When spoken to and encouraged, she 'sang', making up a song of conversation on the spot, some of it rhyming. I didn't get a chance to write any of it down, as it suddenly poured out without warning, but it was mostly about how happy she is to be at the Centre and how much she loves her friends there. A lot of it was about how she hopes she's doing everything right and not offending anyone. She's very diffident and appreciative to the point of servility, this sometimes comes with dementia instead of aggression, through a fear of doing 'the wrong thing'. But she's very happy and cheerful and enjoyed attention. I spoke to her carer later, who came to take her home. She told me Pearl used to be a writer, she wrote books, and for women's magazines. She was the daughter of a major. Now widowed, she's all alone but for her carer and the Centre. Pearl was very happy sitting with the men and listening to them talking. She's a man's woman, said her carer, maybe it reminds her of her married days. She had no children. Her carer has looked after her for nine years. Before that, she sat every day in her bay window in a chair, all alone with no company, hour after hour, day after day, this intelligent communicative woman. She was coherent enough then to report her previous (non DCP) carer was cruel to her and shouted at her. I found this very hard to hear, she's so tiny and sweet natured, just the type a sadist and bully would enjoy targeting. She now has her carer coming in each day to get her up and to bed and meals, and for three days a week she's at the centre. She has very short, standy- up white hair, and very blue eyes, she's very small and thin, like a little white mouse. She has one very bent leg and the other much shorter, walking with great difficulty on a wheeled walking frame. She told me her carer would be coming to pick her up, so she did remember this. She made a big impression on me. Her sweetness still so much there, her creativity still surviving in her 'songs', her vulnerability.

IVY
Constantly walking, greeting, and smiling as long as she keeps in motion.
(DCP Centre)

Ivy has advanced dementia, she walks around constantly, can't stay still and has to be watched to make sure she eats anything at all. She is very thin and small with hunched posture. She carries a plastic baby doll everywhere with her, which she calls 'me babby'. She talks to the staff and others continually, making sociable comments, and everyone is very kind to her. She is always smiling when she is on the move, greeting everyone cheerfully as she passes them over and over again, 'Hello! How are you, lovely to see you, you alright?' I sat with her at cup of tea and cake time. I observed, that whenever she stops moving and being 'busy', her eyes fill with tears and she looks panic-stricken and very sad. It occurs to me she may keep moving to keep this at bay, the realisation of what's happening to her, maybe on some level she understands it.

It would be easy to assume she believes her 'baby' is real, but I don't think she does. She put him down for a minute and I picked him up and asked about him, she said, 'oh, he's lovely' but when I asked his name she said 'it hasn't got one.' Bearing in mind that some 'normal' women nowadays buy expensive customised life-like baby dolls and take them out to shops, instead of having a real baby, this doesn't seem as eccentric or 'demented' as it might once have done. It reminded me of my own ever-moving mother when she had dementia, keeping busy, carrying a bag, or blankets about and repeatedly folding them, obsessively wrapping things in newspaper or anything to hand. It seemed to me Ivy might carry the doll for simple comfort, rather than delusion – to many women, the heft of a baby in her arms would be comforting in an atavistic way, just the feel of it. Something to form a focus, a centre, in a confused chaos. Another insulation against panic terror at how her world has changed and seems to make no sense.

There's something very movingly heroic about how this woman keeps on cheerfully walking, talking, being busy, day in, day out, worn to a blade by perpetual motion.

SADIE
Hospital patient, with dementia and orthopaedic injuries, with a wicked sense of humour.

I met Sadie when she'd just been admitted, and reportedly was finding it hard to lose her autonomy and freedom of choice. Her dementia made it harder for her to remember why she had to be in the ward. She was cross with staff doing things for her. She wanted to be at home so I asked her what she would be doing at home and wrote a poem for her using her answers. We had a laugh together. I felt it helped her maintain her memory of her normal life to have a poem about it to keep.

My Fire.

If I was home, I'd make a fire,
First thing every morning! With
Screwed up newspaper, sticks,
Until the coal catches fire
And starts to glow. Then
I'd sit near the fire, on my
Green velvet chair, with my
Typhoo tea: it's in a plain white
Mug, a mug like me! Milk,
Three sugars, and a slice
Of white toast, with Lurpak on.
I'll read my paper, look to see
How much money someone's left me!
If it's a lot, I'll go to Jersey,
And sit on the beach, nice and easy.

By my fire, though the rain is lashing
Down outside, I'd feel smashing!

The following week, I took her the laminated poem. She didn't remember me or doing it, but she enjoyed the poem and recognised herself in it. She put it under her pillow. She hated being in hospital and longed for home. She had a wicked sense of humour and liked to joke, and made rude remarks about passing staff and patients to me! I asked her what she'd do if she could have anything at all, if she was boss of the hospital, we went through food, drink, view, flowers... We had another good laugh. I wrote her this poem, which shows her fierce and racy character.

IF I WAS IN CHARGE…

I'm tired, I'm hungry, and I want
 To go home! But If I was in charge,
I'd have a drop of whisky, any way,
I'm not fussy! And a nice crab
To eat, with vinegar, and white bread,
Like the crabs I used to buy
At the Market. I'd have tulips and roses,
In a vase, and a rich man - John Wayne
In this bed here, he's smashing!
There's not much room but I
Can always get on top! He could
Bring his horse - or cow, I don't care
What he's got, isn't he lovely?
We'd listen to Bing Crosby, his voice
Sounds lovely, so romantic, I used
To see all his films at the Gaumont
When I was courting. And the view,
I'd have a view of Blackpool, where
I used to play bingo, the beach,
The tower. But for now, a cup of
Hot sweet tea would be nice!

I went away and wrote and typed out and laminated this poem for Sadie and went
back later the same day. She had already forgotten doing the piece and talking to
me, she was quite shocked by what she'd said about John Wayne! But she
laughed about it too.

ROSE

Aged 92, hospital patient, in her final days, thinking of nature,
beauty and kindness.

I: DEBRIDEMENT

Her notes say 'debridement': stripping away dead tissue
From an infected wound. And this high bed is the antithesis
Of a bridal couch. It holds her as if digesting her, absorbing
Her flesh through sucking tubes, leaving her light as a dry fly's
Husk. While its loud cheyne-stokes snorting drowns out
Her fluttering breaths, her brain debrides her from within,
Peeling away the wife, mother, daughter, friend, she was,
As her experiences, passions, are nibbled away by
Dementia's maggot.

I am here to write for this woman whose pale eyes
Are unseeing slits, whose mouth hangs open, soft and toothless.
I sit a long time by her huge and greedy bed as she dies by inches,
Feeling the peace that emanates from her. She is teaching me already
About acceptance, the strength that comes beyond what we call
Dignity. Her face is radiant, calm, relaxed. She mutters
Random phrases, timed to a rhythm as if conversing. I begin
To respond, ask quiet questions, between her phrases, antiphonally.
And she begins to answer.

'Do you have a garden?' *'Yes, I have a garden.'*
'What kind of garden?' *'It's just a casual garden.'*

In that toxic box, nothing thrives but flesh-eating bacteria;
No flowers, no sky, no rain, no sound of nature,
No colour, no scents, no fruit, no music, all,
Ironically, banished in the name of sterility.

Between us, we conjure up her garden, write poetry.

II: CASUAL GARDEN

(written for Rose, on her deathbed)

Slowly, words emerge from her,
Like earthworms after rain.

Yes, I have a garden.
It's just a casual garden,
Mainly plants, trees,
A big lawn, and one at the back.
I put a lot of bushes in, alpines,
All colours. Trees - apple trees,
Flowering blossom trees, a tree
That does coloured leaves.
I used to grow thousands of flowers
In my garden. I owe the lady
Opposite, she helped me
With my garden. I appreciate
What she did. I love my garden.
I hear birds - doves,
Blackbirds. I can smell perfume.

Kindness, love, birds, flowers,
The last things on her mind.

III: SHARING POETRY

A week later, she's still there, but silent.
She's past responding, says the nurse;
When I show her Rose's poem, 'She said all that?'
We agree you can somehow tell
She is a lovely person. I read her the poem.
She does not move. Then I say I'll have to go,
And her face tenses slowly, her lips move,
And clearly, she mouths, 'Thank you.'

Another week on, she's on morphine, but
She opens her eyes, closes her mouth, as
I play birdsong on CD. Robins and blackbirds
Fill the room, pecking up maggots and microbes,
Turning them into song, debriding the dead air
She has to die in. We sit a while in the bird-washed
Room, then I say goodbye, and leave.

A few days later, she is dead. The poem
Stands on the windowsill in place of a view.

CHAPTER NINE
MOVING ACCOUNTS -
FROM OVERSEAS, TO A NEW LIFE OVER HERE

Many older people began life in different countries, came to the UK for varying reasons, and made a life here, often beginning with nothing in a very different culture. Here are three such people: from India, from Trinidad, and from Hitler's Germany.

MARY ISAAC

Childhood in India, visually impaired. After a shock arranged marriage, moved to the UK for a long career, now a user of technology to cope with her disability. (AC Centre)

I'll be 86 in October. I'm registered visually impaired, so instead of reading, I listen to tapes or CDs, or use the computer. I have spoken software, 'Guide'. I've been doing a computer course for five years, with the Blind Society in Newcastle. Social Services introduced me to a luncheon club, where I heard about computer training, and went along. When I started it, it seemed quite complicated, I went every Tuesday morning until I just stopped this year. I can use email, and can write, and listen to files.

I was born in Kerala, in South India, a tourist area, quite beautiful – coconut palms, mango trees, bananas, cashews. We lived very close to the lake, which ran into the sea, so we had water, though we had a hot season as well. We had a big compound! Our family house, our plants, trees, vegetables, a pond, and a pond for fish for us to eat. When I was two and a half or three, I had chicken pox, and my eyes closed up for some days, my retinas were damaged, and that's when it started, problems with my eyesight. I was very short-sighted. When I was in school, I had to sit near the front, with the boys, to see the board but it was still very difficult. When I was 7, my father took me to an optician, we had to travel and stay in a hotel for the night, the optician was English and he had to order my spectacles from England. India was still under British rule then. All our schooling past age 11 was in English. My first language is Malayalam, a sister language to Tamil, they are both connected to ancient Sanskrit. So I grew up speaking two languages. I still have an Indian accent now. We had a lovely childhood. My parents were kind. My father was ever so loving and affectionate.

My mother was good, but a disciplinarian, she overruled everybody, a real matriarch. She was an embroidery and sewing teacher before she married so she made us beautiful clothes. There were five of us girls, and we had the same material and style clothes, when we went to church every week people used to look at us to see what we were wearing this time! It was the Church of England with the same hymn tunes, but translated into our language. Yes, my family were Christian, back to my grandparents' generation. Most people were Hindu, some were Muslim. But Christians were in India long before the British came. Since the Roman times! The first Christians came then, escaping from Jerusalem, St Thomas (yes, Doubting Thomas!) and others came to India through the Khyber Pass, along the old Spice Route, that was orthodox Christianity like Russian Orthodox, chanting, incense, very 'high'. I was the eldest, then four sisters, and one brother, the youngest. I still have two sisters living in India, one of them is still in the same family house I grew up in. She had fever at four years old, polio, and couldn't move – she was paralysed, left disabled. Her face is lovely, you can't tell by looking at her face, but she's been in a wheelchair for 35-40 years. My mother cared for her until she herself died. In the meantime, one of my sisters and her husband had studied for degrees in America, and came back, to Madras, to run an orphanage and work as missionaries. Someone brought a girl in, about four and a half, very poor, malnourished, and said her mother had gone, asking if she could bring her daughter to the orphanage. My sister brought her to my mother and disabled sister and they cared for her and gave her vitamins and cod liver oil and she went to school there. My disabled sister adopted her, and she was 17 when my mother died. So another sister came to stay and organised the house for my disabled sister, wheelchair adaptations, and she had to travel by taxi. A young man was always with the taxi driver to help her in and out. My sister and brother in law thought it a good idea for the young man to marry my sister's adopted daughter, an arranged marriage. He was also teaching simple English to children. That couple stayed and care for my sister and are still there in my family house! They have a son and daughter, the son is doing a degree and the daughter is still at school. I last visited about 11 years ago, I used to visit now and again, and I still speak on the phone to them all. I wanted to do well at school but it was hard with my eyesight, and also girls weren't encouraged to do well in those days. Still, I was educated until I was 18. At 13, I (and one of my sisters) were sent to boarding school, I was there for 3 years. This was because my father was then a Forestry Range Officer and travelled for his work, and my mother went with him sometimes. When I was 16, my mother was back in our house, where she stayed, so I came home and went to school there.

Well, my father was a teacher of English at elementary school, (ages 9-11). The school was set up by the CMS, Church Missionary Society. He was married to his first wife, and he had three children, but his wife died in childbirth with the third, so his parents cared for the children. The First World War came, so my father went to the war. He trained in the army and his battalion went to Mesopotamia, now called Iraq. They waited to be sent to the front, but the war ended and he came back and trained for the Forestry. His job as Forest Range Officer was a very very responsible and good job. Then he married my mother. My half sisters and half brother were then in their teens. My parents were responsible for them, yes so there were nine of us eventually, and the girls went to boarding school. The boy came to live with us and my father was very ambitious for him but he went to different schools and didn't do so well, perhaps because of all the disruption. My younger brother was only 12 when my father died.

So when I got home from boarding school, my father was thinking of retiring so I went to a local school until I was 18. Now my eyesight caused a lot of trouble with families considering an arranged marriage. My parents had great trouble finding me a husband! Families would look into another family's whole history and everything. There was this young man, his family sent him to University, he was intelligent but mucked around and didn't do much work and was having some trouble after two years. His family asked my father for help, he paid for the young man to stay at university and he came to our house for holidays. He wasn't doing too well, anyway his family suggested we marry. I knew nothing about it! He joined the Air Force, the British and Indian Air Force were still one. He came for a holiday, and suddenly, it was all organised! I had no say! I was surprised, and so was my mother! We never heard my parents argue, but I overheard the truth, my father saying something about it, and that's how I knew. 2-3 weeks later, we were married. Well in those days we girls never met boys, we had nothing to do with them. They were kept separate in the house. I had no idea about sex or anything like that. I had met him when he was staying, and he seemed quite pleasant. We were married by special license, we had five days together at my parents' house,and then he was sent to North India with the Air Force and I was left behind at home. It was a shock, staying five days with someone, I felt – 'is that it?!' No privacy, no emotional bond. We married in 1943, and he died two years ago. We got used to each other. He was kind and never raised his voice to me but he was totally irresponsible. After the Air Force, six months after my father died, he came back and I got pregnant with my little girl. So she was born in India. But then suddenly, we were both recruited as teachers in Ethiopia, Addis Abbaba, when she was 5 and a half months old. We were all flown in 2 special planes from Bombay. We were there for 13 years, and my two sons were born there. They kept renewing our contracts every four years but then after twelve years we had another shock when they ended. My husband wanted to be a journalist, he suggested he go to Bombay and I go home to mother! I thought and prayed and decided, that's not on! I'm not going back to mother. I'm an assistant teacher. I took charge. I told him we were going to the British Embassy, I didn't tell him why, he had no idea what was in my mind. He protested, but I insisted. I said, this one thing, I have to do. We had British passports but he'd changed them into Indian ones, he did things like that. But there was no restriction on coming here then anyway. So I went to the Embassy, I'd been there before with sewing groups, and asked them about coming to England. They said yes, but to send him first to find a job and a flat, or it would be hard arriving in a new country with three children otherwise. So he went on his own first, 1958, and found a library job in Streatham. The school where I taught said they were making a dormitory for girls, and I could have a part of it to live in with my children, and get paid, while my husband was in England. Then in 1960, I joined him. Well at first it was terrible! Very difficult, especially with my eyesight. But we had friends from Ethiopia in Birmingham who helped and gave advice, like bringing socks and warm clothes to wear, and a friend in Essex. When I came here we went to church, the Church of England near us, but they were very unfriendly and stuffy and we sat in the wrong pews and were told to move. I said to my husband, I'm not going back there! We went to the Methodist church, on the other side of us, also very near, they were all staring at us as we arrived and went up the steps, the only Indians there. But they were so happy and friendly! 'Are you managing, do you need any help', and they invited us and the children could go to Sunday school. Yes the weather was very cold! Our children were very excited about Christmas as we'd never seen snow.

My children did very well at school and got good jobs and I have grandchildren. I live with my eldest daughter, for ten years now. I had heart trouble, and had a heart bypass operation, but my husband wouldn't move from London! In fact he wanted to go back to India. So I moved up here to Newcastle to be with my daughter and son in law, so we were separated, though he came to visit. I used to phone him every day in London, and every week when he moved to India. He died there.

Now, I listen to library books from the RNIB on CDs. I also belong to a befriending group run by them. We all stay in our houses all over the country, and talk to each other on the phone, like a conference call, arranged through the RNIB's connection. I come to centres like this one at Age Concern. I was doing my computer course. I try my best to be happy! I live with my daughter and I wonder, am I in the way? Am I doing enough? So I look after myself as much as possible. I made up my mind to do as much as possible to occupy myself. My sight is the problem. Though I've also had cancer, as well as heart trouble, and have lymph oedema in my arm, and use a stick to walk.

If you send me my story by email, I'll be able to listen to it. I've wanted to write my story for a long time so I might expand what you write.

CECIL GLADSTONE HUGGINS, 89

Trinidadian, came to UK in the 50s, electrician who worked his way up to build his own house.

He'll be 90 in December. He still lives in a three bedroomed detached bungalow which he built himself, after working for years and living in caravans and a poor council estate to get the money together. He still has a strong Trinidad accent.

CECIL'S STORY.

In Trinidad I worked in the oil field as an apprentice electrician, then for a short time when war began working at the American airbase for six months. Then I lived at San Fernando and worked as an electrician and switchboard operator at the power station and the TPD oilfield. TPD gave me a house in Palseco. I was quite well off then! I paid a shilling a year rent, and they paid all my bills and provided everything. I was married by then, to Cynthia Victorlene and we began to have children. I met Cynthia when I was working in San Fernando, she used to pass my work every day on her way to work at Imperial Stores. First time I saw her I said to my friend, that's the girl I'm going to marry. He said who is she? I said I don't know yet! I asked around and found out she liked to dance, so I went to a dance: I knew she'd be there. I introduced myself and asked if I could walk her home and she said yes. She was seven years younger than I was. So after a while with the San Fernando borough council I heard they were looking for switchboard operators and I went to the oil field with Cynthia. We had married quarters. Our first children were born in the oil field. It was about eight miles from the beach. It was very green, the two boys played in the sugar cane fields. We had chickens, and vegetables, a pumpkin tree, we grew yams and 'dashin', which is like cassava, we had plantains, mangos, bananas. My mother had a banana tree, which my sister Norma still has now. We were quite well off. But I felt I couldn't get any further in my job. And I wanted my children to have the chance of qualifications. Trinidad schools were good but for qualifications at university you had to be up here. So I had an apprentice of mine who'd come up to England and I asked him about coming up. Cynthia was two months pregnant with our third child, our first daughter, when I came up to find a job, leaving the family behind. My apprentice said 'don't do it! You're better off there in Trinidad!' and Cynthia threatened to stay behind! She was a very strong woman. But in this one thing I had my way. She couldn't stay with three children to look after! I felt that if I was there too with my children I could make sure they got qualifications.

I myself wasn't too good at school. It was a boys' RC school. I was clever with my hands but I think a bit dyslexic. They ignored me at school most times. When I was a boy, a tyre rolled off a truck and hit me. I just got up and went on to school, but when I got home that night, I started to black out. I became very ill. I was at home in bed for about a year! I could hardly move without getting giddy. My head would spin, and I saw the furniture fighting and things like that. Eventually I got up and started going to school but I never did well after that. I had a happy childhood though. My mother was Millicent Bartholemew, a very hard worker. She was a negress (sic). My father was called Kang, he was Chinese. All the races mixed in Trinidad, there was no trouble about it, though the Indians liked to keep themselves to themselves. My father had a Chinese surname but my mother made him change it to Huggins before she'd marry him. My father was kind and affectionate but he was a drinker, he liked rum, and a gambler, and he lost his businesses through that. He'd had two or three shops. My mother put him out eventually but she must have put up with him a long time, as my wife knew him. Sometimes he worked in the oil field, and my mother would send my big sister to meet him on pay day to try and stop him drinking it away before he got home.

My mother had thirteen children, some died though and nine grew up. I was the middle child and the first boy. I still have one brother alive, Hugo, here in England, and three sisters in Trinidad. Norma, 96, is the eldest, then Ena, and Violet the youngest. Ena and I looked the most Chinese and so a neighbour gave us Chinese names which stuck, everyone there called me Chin Pun and they still do! They don't know me as Cecil. My father liked rum to drink, and pepper in his food, chillis, I got those tastes from him! I still eat a lot of chillis. I used to drink a lot when I was younger but then my father died from it and so did his brother in law. My father died before my first child was born. Cynthia never said to stop but I didn't want to die like him and I had children so I just stopped drinking a lot. I still like a drink now and then. I knew when to stop when I went out with my friends. Sagar boys, they called us then, in Trinidad, young men who hung out together and dressed in a certain way, very smartly in suits. There were also the 'Coffee Street boys'.

(NOTE: Cecil is still very dapper, and his early photos show him very suavely dressed.)

As a young man I liked to sing and I still do, and I love opera. We had a glee club, and mother made me join the church choir. We gave concerts. I sang a bit in the UK too, with an ex-servicemens' club and we'd go entertaining old people or schools or even prisons. I sang solos. I sing while I'm cooking now. I make spicy stews Caribbean style with lots of chilli and garlic and pork, red beans, rice and peas and so on. I taught my wife Cynthia to cook! I learned from my mother, while Cynthia was an orphan who lived with an aunt. Her parents died when she was small so she didn't know much about them. When we married I made a mistake, I said, stop working, I'll take care of you! So in Trinidad she didn't work outside the home, but she worked very hard up here even with five children.

So, I came up and she stayed in Trinidad, our first daughter was born there and came up here as a baby. Our sons were 6 and 4 when we came up. The nearest university was in Jamaica and we in Trinidad didn't like Jamaica. So it had to be here! I wanted my children to do better than I did.

I had a British passport. I got a job lined up here before I left Trinidad. My ex apprentice here, got me a job, though he said why give up a good job with no bills to pay! He got me a job with a firm of electrical contractors . They were submitting for a big job to build council houses and they even kept the job for a month for me until I got here. There was a lot of work then. I reached Oxford at 8pm one night in November and at 8am next morning, I started work. I found it very cold! I stayed a week in his lodgings and then went into a hostel, like a barracks. I was the only coloured boy there, they were mostly English or Poles come over during or after the war – all the carpenters were Polish. I wanted to go home! In Trinidad, most of the oil field workers were white English. My sister

Violet, now a nurse superintendent, in charge of all the nurses in Trinidad, she paid to help me bring the family over, and I sold my car there and used that money too. When Cynthia, the boys and baby girl got here, we moved into a caravan! It belonged to a man from the Carribbean. We lived in that for a year or so in all weathers, two bedrooms, using shared toilets and bathrooms on the site. Then we moved into a bigger one which was ours. We had to pay bills and things were more expensive here, so although I got paid more, we were worse off than in Trinidad! So I was wiring council houses, as foreman of the electrical department, on a new estate being built, and I asked my boss if I could have a council house. He went and saw the council and told them I'd leave if I didn't get one, so I got a house, on Blackbird Leys. (NOTE: this became a notorious council estate, difficult for the two eldest sons who were identified as gifted and sent to public schools on a special scholarship scheme!) I also worked at Churchill Hospital after that job ended. There was a postman who delivered there and he asked Cynthia if we'd be interested in joining a group of ten families who were going to build their own houses. I said yes! I was treasurer, and electrician. We all paid 2/6 per week for a year and got the land and got started building, sharing our skills. We had two carpenters, four brickies, labourers, a plumber/gas fitter who was the chair of the group. He got an architect to design the houses. We decided to have bungalows. After the Churchill job, I went to work at RAF Abingdon. We've been in this house ever since, I think it was 1976 it was built. Our third son and second daughter were born in Blackbird Leys, so we had five children. Cynthia started to work when we were there. She became a nurse, she walked five miles to work every day. We both worked shifts and I shared the childcare, and the children cared for each other too. Our eldest son did a lot of childcare.

Both me and Cynthia kept working until she became ill with diabetes. She became disabled and lost her sight, she was in a wheelchair, for 5 or 6 years. It crept up on her. I looked after her for the years she was disabled. She died in 2002.

So we brought up five children and worked very hard. I got leukaemia while working on the air base, so they retired me at 64. I was in hospital for a long time, but I got better! This was before Cynthia was ill. I got prostate cancer as well, that seemed to get better as well, and one kidney's gone, but I'm pretty good for 89! I seem to have stabilised. I take care of myself, I exercise, sing opera a lot, cook, with lots of spices! We bring back chilli and hot pepper sauce from Trinidad. I have visited over the years, I went last winter but I think that was my last trip. I visited my sisters, Violet who did very well as nurse superintendent, lives in a street named after her – Lines Lane. She married a

Cecil

doctor. My two eldest boys were identified as gifted and went to boarding school but as day boys. (Silesian College). The eldest has a doctorate and his own computer business, he used to teach: the next became an accountant. My youngest son is a mechanic, my eldest daughter is a nurse, she lectures in nursing. The youngest works in a prison as a warder and nurse.

My life now? it's alright, but sometimes I feel I have done nothing to be proud of. I'm still glad I came to England. I never experienced any racism myself, every place I worked they seemed to like me! They'd say, send for Cecil – they'd ax for me! When I worked for the RAF, the commanding officer asked me to wire his house.

My eldest son lives with me now. My second son used to come every Saturday, and mow the lawn, and spend time, but very sadly he died of cancer not long ago. You aren't supposed to outlive your children. I miss him a lot.

I had a very happy marriage. I still see my family a lot, I have 19 or 20 grandchildren and great grandchildren.

(NOTE:The next day Cecil was dancing (and really well too!) at his granddaughter's wedding, and sitting with his brother Hugo surrounded by many many of their three generations of descendants of all ages and all ethnicities.)

INGE, 90

Jewish refugee from Hitler's Germany. After war experiences there and here, became successful businesswoman in family weaving mill, lives independently after years caring for her late husband.

I came to England with my parents in July 1938, to escape Hitler. We got out just in time, as people were being arrested then. I was 16. My family were Jewish, but we didn't practice the religion. Like many other people, my father kept saying, 'Hitler can't last'. But things got worse and worse for Jews. At the very last minute we got out. My father sold his business cheap to someone. You needed an entry visa to get into England. A good friend of my family in England had a big carpet import warehouse, he used to do business with my father, and he sent us affidavits, which meant we could come over. It saved our lives. My grandmother, aunt and cousin in Germany were sent to death camps and killed after we left. We got affidavits for them too, but they decided to stay behind as my cousin had a fiancé and was going to marry. Then it was too late for them to escape. We took a train from Germany through Holland, crossed the Channel, and stayed in London for six weeks. There were a few places which were depressed areas where we refugees could get work permits and one of them was Gateshead, what's now the Team Valley Trading Estate. Then it was lots of little factories. So we moved to Gateshead and set up a new business to start again from nothing.

In Germany we'd been quite well off. My father had worked hard and built up his own business, he had big carpet and curtain shops and we lived in a nice house in an affluent suburb of Berlin. I mixed with non-Jewish friends and there was no bad feeling at all until after Hitler came to power. We always had a very mixed society, more than here! There were hardly any Jews where we lived. I went to a good school with all my friends, but then when I was 15 the Nazis made me leave school, because my family was Jewish, and go to a domestic school to learn to be a servant! It was a very Jewish school and I found it very hard, I'd never been kosher or anything like that. I was singled out to leave school, none of my non-Jewish friends had to. My friends didn't turn on me, even at the end, despite all the Nazi propaganda and anti-Jewish laws. But I had no proper education after that. After the war, the German government paid me £200 as compensation for depriving me of my education!

I don't usually talk about those times, only now because you are asking about it. Some people revel in all this, I'm a very positive person – I've drawn a line under it. People I've known here who came from Germany are very nostalgic about it but I was different. I thought, you can't go through life being miserable and bringing your children up to be miserable.

We brought to England what money we could get together, we sold some valuable paintings, we had a Corot I remember. And we brought a few things, but we had to start all over again in England. When my children would moan and groan about how they'd like to retire, I'd say, you don't know what hard work is! My father set up a weaving mill, and he and I worked in it. I learned the hard way how to weave. I worked dayshift and nightshift, I was jack of all trades! Me, my father and four girls I trained to be weavers, made furnishing fabrics, in what was then modern 'Scandinavian' style. A fabric designer, Bernard Klein, came to work with us. During the war we made army blankets, we'd set up the mill just before war broke out. After the war the business got bigger and bigger and did very well.

My sister left Germany too but she was engaged and her fiancé was from Argentina so they both went there. We were very close but I didn't see her for years, until 1949. My brother came over to England two or three years before us. Things in Germany were already dicey. He got a job here until war broke out. He was only too happy to join the forces, the Special Pioneer Corps, against Germany. His language ability was very useful and he ended up in the Intelligence Service. We never found out much about it, but he died at only 41 and no-one would tell us what he died of, but I think it was connected to what he saw and did. My sister in law, his wife, never spoke of it, even though we went to his funeral. Hardest thing I ever did, was telling my parents he'd died. His wife is now 96 and lives in London. We get on well now but we didn't then!

It's all so long ago, it's best left alone. So I don't ask her now either.

When I came to England, we found people here very kind and welcoming, they all knew we were refugees. I had learned English at school, and so had my mother, but my father had to learn fast! I made friends easily and immediately found a 'best' girlfriend.

Then I met my husband, he was Hungarian. He had no family of his own. He was on holiday in England when war broke out and he joined my brother's corps, and later the artillery. When my brother was in the forces during the war, he brought him to stay with us when they were on leave, and he and I just clicked. He went off to do a course in Bradford, a three year course in one year, at a technical college, and then he came and joined our family firm after we married. When my father died, my husband took over and built up the business to something really big. We had a lovely house in Embleton, 300 years old. We married in March 1944, he had embarkation leave. He was in France, he was at Dunkirk in 1941. We were married for 57 years. We spoke English even when we were alone. You didn't speak German during the war! Since my mother died I have nobody to speak German to. You *can* forget your mother tongue. I spoke to a friend in Switzerland recently and I was searching for the words.

I went back to Germany after the war, in 1952, seven years after the war ended. The place was in bits, with bomb damage. It meant nothing to me. I looked at where we had lived, it left me absolutely cold. Our big house was now flats. Our firm had an agent in Germany and it turned out he lived in those flats! He insisted I came to see it. I wanted to remember how it had been inside, so I wouldn't go in.

I have three daughters. Two married non-Jews, one did but he's not religious. My 6 grandchildren and 9 great grandchildren don't have a clue about it!

My husband died 12 years ago. I miss him as much now as I did then. I had a friend, she said she'd been a widow 20 years, it gets no better. He was ill for 12 years with cancer. He was very positive, he'd say let's go on holiday! If he felt better. I nursed him all that time. He was in the Marie Curie hospice for three months, but then he felt better and came home, he lived three more years. But I could always tell. On holiday in Majorca, he swam every day but then one day he didn't want to, and I knew. He was only in hospital 24 hours before he died in the RVI. I was prepared, but the shock comes after. The first two years were awful, I had to really fight with myself, but now I only have good memories of him. We loved our old house by the sea, I love living in the country, but when he became ill we moved here to be near the hospital for all his treatments. This is the nearest thing to the country in the city. We moved into this high rise flat, it has a wonderful view of fields, and cows, and trees. But I'm not made for flat-living! I don't like living here but it's safe and convenient. I wish I hadn't sold my house. But I have a balcony and I garden on it, it gets a lot of sun.

I live independently, alone since my husband died. I have a cleaner comes once a week. I like to cook for my family and they come to dinner often, they call me meals on wheels!

I still drive my car, a Clio, but I hate motorways. A lorry drove into me last winter which put my confidence back. So no long journeys now, just up the coast to Embleton. I still travel. I've just been on a cruise on my own. I don't like airports now. This cruise went from North Shields, a Baltic cruise to St Petersburg in Russia. Last year I went to Norway. I met a very nice lady from South Shields, I still see her. She's young, 83. I met some nice people this year but I fell into a bus! I was black and blue and bleeding. I had a mini-stroke two years ago, which means I can't hold a pen properly. I can't read my own shopping lists! I get to know lots of nice people, and people in these flats. A man downstairs rings me to see if I'm alright if he doesn't see me about for a day or so. But at my age, you make acquaintances, not really friends. You don't have that shared history. Luckily I'm a person who can always find something to do. I have many modern novels which I read, my daughter passes them on to me, she's in a reading group. I keep up to date. I don't keep them though, I don't want one more photo or book or ornament! I have a Kindle too, which I use a lot. I love the theatre. I go with my daughter. Your pals aren't there when you outlive your generation. I said to the doctor, I can't do what I used to do, he said for a little old lady you don't do badly. I said, is that all you can do for me?! When I had my stroke, my hairdresser who comes to the flat saw me on the floor, and she knew what it was – she used to volunteer at a Stroke Centre so I was lucky. I'd had no warning, except I kept dropping things, a letter, a cup of tea, just before. I love paintings. I have a painting of my mother done when she was about fifty. I have three Norman

Cornish paintings, I love his work! I bought them years ago and also gave some to my daughters (*one is dated 1960: a miner's portrait, a night scene at the pit*). This one's my favourite! (*a horse and cart with some cheeky children looking over the back*) it reminds me of my grandchildren! This lamp we brought with us from Germany. Look at his face! (*it's a bronze statue of an old man in clogs, carrying a lamp. He looks uncannily like a Norman Cornish north east pitman!*)

I'm not worried about dying. I'd like to go to bed and not wake up. My idea of heaven! I have no regrets at all. I have wonderful memories. Not many people can say that.

NOTE: Inge is tiny, her hair is up in a neat French pleat, back from her fine drawn, aquiline features. She wears tasteful gold jewellery. The portrait of her mother on the wall is by Eugen Spiro. Struck by this lovely picture I looked him up to find he was a Jewish artist who also fled from Hitler, to the US, where he painted Einstein!

Inge, before Hitler destroyed her world.

Inge today

CHAPTER TEN
YOUNG MINDS, IMAGINING OLD AGE

THE OLD AGE THE YOUNG WOULD LIKE FOR THEMSELVES, FAR INTO THE FUTURE.

Encouraging the students to think the unthinkable, that they might themselves one day grow old, produced a strange mixture of pieces and poems. Freedom was a strong unifying theme, freedom from rules and bossy adults and responsibilities, to behave as badly as you like – but at the same time, a strong disinclination to behave in a stereotyped 'old' manner, was clear. A life of hedonistic pleasure and idleness, or frantic sport and adventure, was a common mixture. This leads to some strange combinations, where a life of junk food and laziness can also involve youthful looks and energetic mountain climbing! Some wish to make the world a better place. Some clearly wish to be like their own caring grandparents, spoiling and spending time with their own grandchildren in their turn. However, it's interesting that many young people rebel against the very stereotypes they listed in Chapter One.

First, the Year Seven students.

WHEN I GROW OLD
Millie Elsdon

To sum it up, I really won't care!
About what people think about me or the types of
clothes I'll wear!
I'll travel the world, visit places far and wide
Swim with dolphins, maybe surf a large tide

129

Try exotic foods, never tasted before
Maybe some I'd digest, and be left wanting more
Snails, brains and frogs legs too,
All of these things, youth wouldn't dare to do

I'll wear what I think looks good on me
I won't really care what others see
Long, brown ankle skirt,
And shoes I could wear, that wouldn't hurt

No! I wouldn't want to dress like that,
I would never dare wear a feathered hat!
Skinny jeans with cool white plimsolls
I will never go to Greggs to buy sausage rolls.

I'll be my own person, and only live to impress
Me! As I'm the one that truly knows me best!

WHEN I'M OLDER
Thomas Collins

When I'm older
I will walk for a charity
When I'm older
I will climb Mount Everest
When I'm older
I will swim the English Channel
When I'm older
I will help the schools around me
When I'm older
I will travel the world to help the people

When I'm older
I will fight the enemies to help the police
After all this I'll have a pint at the pub
This is when I'm older.

WHEN I GET OLDER . . . .
Emily Jane Thielmann

When I get older,
I will look after my grandchildren,
Taking them the places my nana took me,
Giving them pocket money and buying them treats with
my pension,
Baby sitting them and giving them all the love I have left
in my heart.

When I get older,
I will invite Molly, Ellie, Kaysha and Emily around for
tea and to knit with them talking about the latest
countdown show,
Natter on and on about the good old days,
When we were young and wild,
Going to clubs and partying all night long.

When I get older,
I will still go out and go wild but only on special
occasions,
I will drink and dance being careful not to do in my hip,
Go to the bingo with my mates,

And that's who I want to be! ☺

WHEN I AM OLD
Alicia Hansen

When I'm old I would like to have done all my goals in life
I would like to cut all the fear out of my life with a knife
I would like to be stylish
And be a little bit childish
Never forgetting the best times of my life
And I would also like to be a wife
With kids and grand kids
Just thinking about them while watching Flog It,
'What's the biggest bid?'
I'm not scared about being old
It's a way of life... So I've been told!

And Year Ten:

I WANT TO BE...
Joseph Monaghan

When I am old
I want to be an honest person.
I want to be caring and kind and to have
A good reputation. I want to be known
For being a good person.
I will stay active and go out all the time.
I want to make the most of my life.
Live everyday as if it were my last.
I want to be positive and ambitious,
Have a nice house, somewhere in the countryside
Away from the dangers of the city.

WHEN I AM OLD
Hannah Richardson

When I am old, I want to be active. I would like to travel and go on a lot of relaxing holidays with my husband. I would like to break the stereotypical views and beliefs about old people. Not be seen as grumpy, frumpy, boring stubborn, decrepid and helpless. I want to be still able to be as active and do as much as I do now. Not have to rely on my family and the community to look after me . I want to keep good health not die or be ill with ailments and diseases though I will do what I need to stay healthy. I want to be able to go out with friends, have a good time. Not be held back by my age. I also want grandchildren to look after and spoil which is a contrast to what I have said previously as a more stereotypical trait. I want to be financially stable to not have to live in a rubbish bungalow and not be able to pay for any luxuries I want and for the people around me.

WHEN I AM OLDER
Russell Renton

When I am older I do not want to be a miserable person,
I want to be happy and energetic
And I want to still have a purpose and stay active.
I'll exercise regularly and have a job.
I wouldn't want to be lonely and I will live in a nice modern house,
I hope.
I will have a Newcastle season ticket and go to every match with my friends, who will all be old also,
But the main thing I do not want to be stereotypical.
I wouldn't ask for help and do things for myself and be independent.

WHEN I AM OLD I AM GOING TO...

Jessica Davison

Get my teeth whitened on a regular basis.

Keep fit and do sports such as tennis, swimming and football.

Use antiwrinkle cream and look after my skin

Use a lot of fake tan and keep up with the latest hairstyles and fashion icons

I will go on holiday a lot to places like Benidorm, Australia, Magaluf, Costa del Sol

Go to the pubs and bars a lot

Eat a lot of fatty foods

Have a nice cosy but modern house

Have a nice garden with waterfalls and decorations and mini windmills

Listen to the latest chart music

Learn to cook my own food

Do unusual hobbies like sight-seeing, gather collectables.

WHEN I GET OLD

Jonny Legg

When I am old I want to party all night
And sleep all day.
I want to go out naked in the summer,
I want to watch movies,
Listen to loud music,
And get a tattoo of a skull
On my skull,
I want to go to Las Vegas
And have a butler to make noodles.

I will go to the moon,

Throw food at pigeons,

Climb high mountains,

And walk for miles,

And race around on my mobility scooter.

WHEN I AM OLD...
Shannon Slattery

I will wear mascara and red blush on my cheeks.

I will take fancy holidays every few weeks.

I will learn to cook and knit in my spare time.

I will wear vibrant colours like magenta and lime.

I will have weekly lunches with my old school friends.

We will talk about memories and go on for days on end

I will work part-time, and buy clothes from the high street.

I will cook the grandchildren's tea, and give them jelly sweets.

I will watch daytime telly, and yell at the screen.

I will think about memories, and everything I've seen.

I WANT TO...
Alex Tait

When I am old I want to play bowls and also to go trainspotting. Also I want to travel to different places in the country to collect and observe different kinds of rocks. I will go and watch every Newcastle United game and go to every Ashes cricket game in both England and Australia. I will want to try lots of different foods and different kinds of beer. I also want to grow a handlebar moustache and a fantastic bushy beard which will be dyed black and white.

WHEN I AM OLD I WOULD:

Christian Johnson

Drink when and what I want,
Do what I want,
See who I want,
And just relax.
When I am old I would:
Look like I want,
Dress how I want,
I will:
Ride around on my mobility scooter
And cause havoc!

CHAPTER ELEVEN

DATING AND MATING – a glimpse of sex over seventy

It's common for people of older age groups to consider their sex lives to be deeply private. As I was already asking intimate questions, and listening to all sorts of details of their lives, I chose not to ask anyone directly about the sexual aspects of their current life. Apart from the different attitudes when they were growing up and forming relationships, there is also the inhibiting factor of the way people commonly refer to the idea of older people having sex or even kissing as something to be derided. At the moment, in *The Archers*, two characters, only in their fifties, are becoming romantically involved, and I looked at the online discussion boards to find a barrage of 'gruesome', 'acting like teenagers' and 'old people doing it, yuck' type of comments. This attitude has resulted in more stories in this book of past sexual assault, or abuse, than happy sex lives. However, two interviewees voluntarily brought up the subject, so I'm placing them here, brief as they are, with no comment about whether they stand alone or are part of a longer interview extracted from elsewhere in the book. I have no reason to suppose these are isolated experiences. I did hear of many older people dating or forming new relationships when widowed or divorced. No doubt some would like to think this is always about 'companionship', just as used to be assumed about people with disabilities, before they began to assert their right to be considered sexual beings. It's harder for older people to follow suit, as they tend to be parents and grandparents, and there is a natural 'ick' factor involved because of that, just as always between the generations.

JAMES

Happily married, in his eighties.

James was talking in the presence of his wife, and was telling me how happy they are, when he added this, with an aside to her,

> 'In fact, we've a nice little sex life, don't we, pet? You see I'm very lucky, my wife is very attractive, and I'm proud to be seen out with her.'

Indeed they were both attractive people, well dressed and stylish.

PAULINE, AGED 77

Talks of dating and sex after 70.

Pauline was widowed and over a decade later began dating. This is what she said about it.

PAULINE'S STORY:

Dating when you are older, it's nice, it makes a big difference to your life, having someone who'll come and see you, take you out. Yes, other older people have boyfriends, and date. My boyfriend's sister had an unhappy marriage, now she's got a boyfriend, she's around 70. Mine is a romantic relationship. It adds a lot to my life. My cousin said to me, she couldn't be bothered with a man in bed! I said to her, that's the best part! I was on HRT, it makes you feel very randy! I was on it for years. Then this young doctor said we all had to come off it, as it is bad for the heart. I'd rather take the risk! After that I didn't feel like sex so much any more. So we don't now. He's getting older anyway. This young doctor just said, 'After all, you can't stay young forever!' A couple of months later, he dropped down dead playing badminton. So my relationship is more like companionship now. But younger people think you're finished with all that once you get over sixty! I wish I could still be on HRT though!

AUTHOR'S NOTE: Pauline, after a very long hiatus in her sexual life, may have needed the boost of HRT, but couples who are still together after many years may well continue to have an enjoyable sex life well beyond common expectations.

CHAPTER TWELVE

STATE OF INDEPENDENTS – elders are doing it for themselves

Far from being 'dependent on young people' or 'helpless', many older people are still living independent lives, either alone or as couples. The stereotype goes on, because those living quietly in their own homes, minding their own business, are just not known about. The IAH 85+ study, of a large cohort now turning or turned 90, discovered many people at an advanced age, who still drive, who use computers, who pursue hobbies and take exercise, who see a lot of their families but don't rely on them, who are generally healthy, who travel, and who are still working or learning (see 'Earners and Learners' and 'Moving Stories' for more 'Indys', also some are featured in other sections).

ENA, 80
Still swimming, driving, living independently, had two widely different childhoods, one deprived, one cared for, due to wartime evacuation.
Had a successful career well into her 70s.

Ena is 80, slim, slight, tiny and neat, with a smooth silver bob with a hairslide in it. She is dressed in colour coordinated clothes with dangling leaf earrings that match. Ena's story confounds a whole host of stereotypes, and could have been placed in virtually any category in this book!

ENA'S STORY: I live in my own detached bungalow, do my own gardening, and drive my little white Ford Ka. I worked full time from the age of 14, until I was 72! Even after that I still worked freelance, doing cover for staff who were off etc, for some years. Since ten years ago, when I was 70, I go swimming six days a week, at 7 am. I swim 30 lengths. I've always kept fit and I like to start the day with an activity. I really miss it when I'm ill or can't go for some reason. I didn't learn to swim until I was 38!

I had a strange childhood, in two totally different families, because of being evacuated during the War. Until I was eight, I lived with my own family which was poor. I had two brothers and two sisters. My mother wasn't close to us; she wasn't affectionate. When she was dying as an old woman, she said to my sister that she'd loved us, my sister said to me, 'why did she never tell us that before!' My mother had no patience with us and didn't spend any time with us. We were all crowded at home. As for my father, we didn't know much about him, even though he was at home nearly all the time. He never spoke to us, just lolled about like a bear with a sore head, smoking like a chimney, it killed him in the end. He came out of the army, and hardly ever worked, my mother would say, 'Tell yer da to go to work, we've got no money,' but he took no notice. I see men nowadays at the swimming pool with their children, they play with them, dress them, are interested in them, years ago, if you saw a man with a pram outside, it was very unusual. I like to see men now taking part in their children's lives.

But from when I was 8, to when I was 14, I was evacuated to Thornhill in Cumbria, I wasn't missed, and I was much happier there than at home. I had the most beautiful home there and I was like an only child. 'Aunt' Sally was a teacher, and 'Uncle' Isaac had worked in the iron ore mine. She spent time with me, she taught me to sew, and cook, and knit, I liked to help in the house because she made it like a game. I had a little Hoover for the stairs, and I had to iron the hankies and pillowslips but I didn't mind. I had Christmas like I'd never had before – waking up on Christmas day, and there was the Christmas tree with all the things on it! I used to sit on Uncle Isaac's knee and he'd sing 'Londonderry Air'. Aunt Sally used to go to church as she was in the choir, so we'd go three times on Sundays, but I was allowed to come home for some of the time. They were both so kind, but I had to behave. I knew not to ask her for things. She'd come to collect me from school, we only went for half days in war time, with cakes and sandwiches, and take me on the beach for a picnic. You could go on that beach, not like Whitley Bay, which had barbed wire and concrete blocks on it during the war to stop invaders. Uncle Isaac had chickens, and it was my job to go with a bucket and feed them, and collect the eggs, and every week, I went to a cupboard to get my 'wages' for doing it! One of my older sisters was evacuated with me but she was stroppy, and refused to do any chores, or do anything she was told, so she soon went home and I was left there on my own. When we first arrived, we were very shabby, so Aunt Sally took us to the shops in Whitehaven, and bought us tartan skirts, dressing gowns, slippers, all sorts. She taught me a lot. My mother never visited me in six years. She did send me some sweets from the ration, at Christmas and my birthday, and do you know, I never ate them! I kept them to play at shops with the little girl next door. My mother was angry when I came home and still had them! But I still have my own teeth!

So when I was 14 I was forced to come home. I didn't want to, I cried and cried, and so did Aunt Sally. I think my mother wanted me to go to work and so she could get my wages, and of course the war ended. Aunt Sally got breast cancer, she used to rub her side under her breast, I used to wonder why. Nobody told me she was ill, but a lady next door wrote to tell me she'd died. I didn't like it at home, it wasn't well kept. I swore never to live like that. All of us five children did well in the end, strangely. My oldest sister Eunice was like my mother, she cared for me and was the only breadwinner some of the time. And my two brothers pushed me to do well at work. My brother Eric went to Rutherford College, worked at Armstrong's, then he was in the Navy during the war. After that he wanted to be a farmer so he started with one goat! He moved to Richmond and then decided to be a teacher, he ended up a Year Head. My oldest brother Fred went to technical school, and during the war he worked at Parsons Optical Department, he was working on something important for the war, lenses of some kind I think, then he joined the RAF. He ended up working in Australia, on those huge telescope lenses. His wife lives here now though. My oldest sister Eunice went to Edinburgh University, and trained as a pharmacist and did very well. My stroppy sister had three illegitimate babies! Three! At the time that was very scandalous. The first one was to a soldier when she was, I think, 17. Mother pretended not to know about it right till the end, though she always made her leave the house through the back door and go up the back lane so the neighbours wouldn't know. I only knew she'd got fat. Eunice thought my mother planned to 'get rid' of the baby somehow. So she had the baby, a boy, and kept him, because Eunice really liked children. She used to babysit for people to earn pocket money. Oh, I've no idea how his mother felt about it, she never showed any interest in him. Eunice made our mother keep the baby. She cared for him herself when she was home from work and brought baby food and things for him from the pharmacy. When she was at work, mother looked after him, he was in a clothes basket. He grew up and married and they disappeared somewhere but Eunice always kept in touch. Then my sister had a second baby, another boy, this time Eunice arranged for her to go into the Salvation Army place. They persuaded her to give it away. She showed no signs of being upset at all. She had jobs all over the place. Her third baby was by a Polish soldier, a girl, she was adopted too. Funnily enough, when we were all still struggling to make something of ourselves, that sister did the best of any of us! She married a man whose wife died, and she just walked into a lovely house in Richmond, this man really worshipped her. I didn't keep in touch with her, but I was close to the others. Eric's the only one left alive now.

So I did a term or so at school when I got home, and Fred paid for me to do evening classes five evenings a week to make up for the education I'd missed during the war. Our school had no gym, so we'd go to my brother's Technical School to use theirs, in our navy knickers! Their gym had a balcony and the boys would watch us from there! I later married one of them...

At 14, I started work. I went to the labour exchange and they sent me for a job as a welder in a factory. My brothers said you can do better than that! Eunice got me a job as a counter assistant at the chemist's, Mawson Proctors in Grainger Street, Newcastle. The pay was poor. My two ambitious brothers kept helping me do better. One of them told me about a job at a coal company, people bought coal on hire purchase and I did the clerical work. It was a better job but not well paid. Then my brother said I've found you a better job, as a telephonist at a telephone exchange in Carliol Square. So I went there and picked it up just like that! I loved that job! I had such flexible fingers, and it was like I'd been doing it for years, right from the start. After I was married and moved down south, I got a transfer to an area exchange there, then they opened a new one. I got promoted. They needed new telephonists and I got the job of training the new entrants. I did like it! They trained for six weeks. I was always one for Keep Fit, and at a rally a girl came up and said I'd trained her, and she'd wanted to be like me and became an instructor too, that was nice to know. The Telephone service became part of the Civil Service when I was about 16. I kept on working there for 25 or 26 years, but I passed for promotion which would have meant moving. So I applied for early retirement. I needed to care for my husband for a while as he'd had a nervous breakdown. But I kept on working full time as a freelance, 'Implementing Civil Policy', which meant insolvency and receivership work.

When I retired, a big company in the city rang me and asked if I'd cover a maternity leave, full time but self-employed. I said I would, and stayed working for them until I was 72! And then kept doing staff absence cover for a few years more. I always went to Keep Fit two nights a week, and yoga, and I'd taken up swimming when I was 38. I and a friend went with our colleagues to the pool but she and I couldn't swim. Two lads there towed us into the deep end, but then they were sorry and to make up for it they taught us to swim. My husband and I moved house, and I went every Saturday to a family session at the pool. And of course I still go now! When I started going six times a week, swimming 30 lengths of a 33m pool, it took me a while to get to know people but some Indian ladies there spoke to me, and eventually 20 of us got together, we did life saving classes too. We'd all go and have a hot drink afterwards. I found it better to go swimming than just sitting with a cup of tea in my hand at coffee mornings and so on, I'd rather do something, and it gives you all something to talk about. My husband came too.

I met my husband when I was 16, at a dance at the Oxford Galleries in Newcastle, it was an Easter afternoon, it was like a cattle market then, you had to wait to be asked to dance. So David asked me to dance and then to go to the cinema, and he told me he remembered me in my navy gym knickers! He'd just been demobbed from the navy, as a Chief Petty Officer, when we met, he'd worked at Parsons Marine Turbine before that. We married when I was just turned 18, my sister in law found us two rooms in Heaton to live in. Then he became a policeman, and ended up as an Inspector. We were moved about because of his job, before we moved south, we went to Bellingham in Northumberland, I hated it! I worked in Robbs shop for a while then. He was hardly ever around, with shift work. I kept working. I have one son, a grandson and a granddaughter.

My husband died three years ago, after 57 years of marriage. We used to go swimming together. He'd had a hip operation but was recovered, and we went to the pool one Saturday morning, six days after Christmas, it was pouring with rain. He wasn't in long, when he said he felt cold and was getting out. 'I'll wait for you in the car park,' he shouted. I finished my swim with a friend and we walked to the car, and were surprised to see that he was asleep. She said, I'll go round and give him a fright! She opened the door and said, 'Ena, he's dead.' It turned out to be asbestosis from when he worked at Parsons all those years ago. So I have my bungalow, and my garden, and two lovely nieces nearby who visit and take me out and to their houses for Christmas. My granddaughter rings me up. I see my sister in law often as well. I have a Siamese cat called Chang, he's fifteen now. We've always had cats. I'm pretty well, but I sometimes have trouble with my toes, my feet were injured in a bus crash years ago, and they get worse with time. But I keep on swimming!

DAVID, 83 AND MAUREEN, 77

David, a self-made man who strove for an education the hard way: Maureen, widowed young: an independent couple happily married, and a heartwarming ghostly encounter.

I came from a working class family, my parents were proud people but struggled to manage on very little money. But through their support, hard work, and some luck, I'm now, at almost 83, living happily with my wife Maureen, who's 77, in a large detached bungalow with a big back garden overlooking beautiful countryside and near the sea. I'm in good health, and we live independently apart from some paid help with the garden. We socialise a lot, often eat out, walk by the sea regularly, and I still play golf, several times a week, occasionally all 18 holes, usually 14 holes, depending on the weather. I've belonged to voluntary organisations all my working life, and done charity work through them, some of them I've given up now but I'm still active in the Rotary club and support charity work through them. We have five children between us, all doing well, scattered all over the world, so we keep up with them and our six grandchildren by using the computer: emailing, using the internet for research, and talking to our family using skype. We also travel, for holidays and visiting our children. We've just been on a cruise to the Canaries, and we often fly to the USA, we've been seven times, recently to Washington, next it'll be Denver! We visit family in the south of France, Germany, all over, some of them have exotic jobs abroad. We both still drive.

We've been married 32 years, it's my second marriage (I was divorced after 21 years of marriage to my first wife, and my wife was widowed young) and we are very happy.

But it wasn't like this when I was young, growing up with my twin sister. My mother took in paying guests, three cooked meals a day, to make ends meet, and my father was a groundsman for the council, it was an awful job. In the depression after the First World War, when there was widespread unemployment, he'd even gone round clearing snow to make a bit of money. He was a gentle, kind man, and I think being in the trenches in WW1 had a terrible effect on him, though he'd never talk about what he'd seen or been through. You can see the difference in the photos of him. He had no confidence to try to get better jobs as he was afraid of being unemployed like just after the war. My mother worked hard and was brilliant at managing with very little money, and self respect was vital to her. She'd grown up as one of thirteen children with a boozy shipbuilder father and an overworked but very strong mother. She went hungry herself when we were very poor and would chew a few grains of raw rice instead of eating. Her first child died at birth, then a couple of years later she gave birth to us twins, at home, with just a midwife, they couldn't afford a doctor. My sister Sheila and I were close, it was like always having an ally, you know! We were both doing well at school, my sister was maybe brighter, or just a bit ahead like girls often are at that age, but as we came up to high school age, things went very wrong for me. Not long before the grading exam, which decided if you went to grammar school or not, I got an agonising ear condition, which kept me off for weeks, I couldn't eat or sleep and became like skin and bone. A week after I went back to school, the school dentist came, pulled out a tooth, and damaged my jaw so I couldn't eat for two weeks, only a few weeks after that was the exam. I just missed passing by 3 or 4 marks. My twin sister passed so she went to grammar school, I didn't. You can imagine what that felt like.

Of course we had very little money, so my sister had a hard time there with well off peoples' daughters, she had everything second hand and the teachers would mock her in front of the class for having a father who had a humble job.

And I had virtually no education at all after that, there was no academic focus in secondary schools, and then the Second World War started! Teachers under forty were called up, we only had a very few, and we had lessons only three times a week, at our house in fact! We spent most of the week working in allotments! But we had a teacher called Miss Pringle, and she was the one who made the big difference to my life. She said to me, 'you can do a lot better than this, you are capable of doing better than anyone here, IF you choose to!' I was embarrassed, being picked out, but it made me feel there was hope, that someone believed in me. After that I worked harder and was always top. At fourteen, I had to leave school, 1942, with almost no education. My sister at the grammar school couldn't go on to university anyway as we had no money so she got a job at the ministry which she had to leave when she got married! But both of us did well in the end, though we did it the hard way. So there I was, fourteen, needing a job. The headmaster arranged for me and another lad to have an interview at a local estate agents, I got the job as an office boy, probably as I had long pants on and the other lad didn't! I liked the work, I thought, this is great! Measuring houses, putting up signs, that sort of thing.

But I could see I needed to get qualified to get any further, by doing exams with the Institute of Surveyors, but I couldn't even become a student with them unless I had six decent passes in school subjects. This was a big barrier, I had never even done science, or algebra, or a language, so my mother sent away for a correspondence course with Bennett College, which I worked at in the evenings after work. I chose six subjects, and my mother went out cleaning offices as an extra job to pay for it although she was working so hard running the guest house. My sister helped me a lot with the work as well. I passed the six subjects, then had to start studying for my professional qualifications, as a Chartered Surveyor, which by then I could pay for out of my wages, though they were small. I was seventeen. I gave my mother my wages and my sister a bit of pocket money, and my mother gave me a little bit back for spending money, I wanted to contribute to the family. Even before that, when I did a paper round!

But then, at seventeen, I was called up for National Service. The war had ended, but we still had to go, and I joined the Army and did my two years in Inverness and Southampton. I got three shillings a day, I sent half home until I just couldn't afford it, I had to buy extra food as we didn't get enough. I was six foot two and always hungry! I remember coming home, and my Dad coming to meet me off the train, he was nearly in tears when he saw me, and then at home Mum was cooking like mad! When I got home, at twenty, I found that having done my National Service, the government would pay for my studies, and four years of night classes later, I passed my exams. I told the firm I was working for but they weren't interested so I realised I'd have to look elsewhere. Then a big London estate agent opened a Newcastle office, the manager wasn't qualified though he was very experienced, and they needed a qualified surveyor for mortgage valuations. I got the job and did five years there. I was very lucky, I worked with a London team, we dealt with rating appeals for big firms and private schools, I did the rating for Fenwicks, all terrific experience, but I was a very small cog in a big wheel. I got a rise each year but not much, I was ambitious to earn more, I wanted to get married and get a place of my own. I was twenty nine, I wanted to get on.

A surveyor's job came up with a building society, with a car, and a special mortgage deal, which I was offered, so I gave my notice. But then one of two partners in a local firm, rang up and invited me for supper. He'd known me for years. He said he and and his business partner were both getting on, he had no sons and his partner's weren't in the business. Would I be interested in a partnership in the firm? I said yes, it was a fabulous chance! I asked what I'd make. The big ambition then was to make a thousand pounds a year by the time you were thirty. The other job had offered me £1200. He said, in the last year my partnership share would have got me three thousand! I tried not to show my excitement. But I had to buy the partnership, and my share of the premises, furniture, cars, and of course I had no money. My parents had nothing, and I was just getting married, where would I get that? He said, you can buy your share over ten years, out of your wages, with no interest. The other costs, he said they'd raise the mortgage on the premises, to help me. I had to borrow the reduced amount from the bank. The manager said no and made me feel that small. So my new employer handed me some stocks and shares from the safe as security for the loan, I went back and the manager was all over me, 'is that enough you're borrowing?'I got on great with my new firm, in fact my senior partner then gave me half his share of the business. They gave me my head to try new things, like better advertising and marketing, and in two years, I'd doubled their turnover. As the two older partners retired I gradually expanded the business to eight offices and took in four younger partners, eventually increasing the staff from 12 to 67. I was renting a flat in town, already married to my first wife, but now I bought a bungalow, then a big house, at the coast. We had three children, then after our divorce, I was single for 4 years before I met my second wife. While working, I got involved in lots of things. I'd played tennis until I was 35, and on the committee of the tennis club, then I switched to golf, I'm very keen, I had a single figure handicap by I was 40, and became Captain of the Golf Club. I was chairman of the Junior Surveyors, of the Round Table, and Master of the Lodge in the Masons. I also joined a Debating Society, to help with speaking etc.

After the trenches of WW1, in WW2, my father volunteered for the ARP, and ended up in charge of the mortuary where all the bombed bodies were taken. Poor Dad, he was a lovely man, he had horrible jobs, ten pounds a week was the most he earned. He died of lung cancer in his very early sixties. We blame the chemicals they made him use as a groundsman, he'd be spitting up black stuff at nights after work. My mother, a marvellous cook, who had supported me so well, lived into her nineties, and I was able to help support her in her old age. My sister later went to college and became a teacher when her children were older. (Her husband also did night classes to get qualified and promoted and did well too.) Both of us lived in nice detached houses near each other and near my mother, so she could be looked after and we saw a lot of her. Between marriages, I rented a bachelor flat, and one night I was looking through some work papers, concentrating on the work, when suddenly I smelled pipe tobacco smoke in the room, the kind Dad smoked, Erinmore. I looked round, and there he was, sitting on the sofa! I just said, Dad! And he disappeared. I wasn't scared at all, I was so disappointed he couldn't stay longer. Someone once told me it must have been very hard for him to appear like that. I don't know, I don't normally tell people about it. It's funny, because my mother was much more forceful and powerful than him, you'd think it would be her. I've never been interested in such things and would never have expected it to happen. I often wish he'd lived long enough to get the benefit of his children's success.

So life now is good, busy, independent, and fun, and with a family we've been able to support, as my family supported me in every way they could, despite having no money.

JAMES AND DOROTHY, 90 AND 86

Independent lives, computing, grape growing, and making Northumbrian pipes, after lives of work and war service.

Jim is 90, Dorothy is 86. They live together in a large house which they have shared for about 42 years. They are totally independent. They use no cleaners, carers, day centres, and though they have a loving family of children (son and two daughters) and grandchildren, they mostly live too far away to give practical everyday help. They have a conservatory with a well established grapevine in it, with bunches of black grapes hanging. They swap grapes for next door's Bramley apples. The house is full of paintings, mostly by one of their two daughters, who sells her work through a gallery but has a day job. There is one by the other daughter too. There are three portraits by Jim's uncle, showing great promise, cut short when he was killed in WW1.

Jim is red/green colour blind. He's now quite deaf but manages well with his hearing aid and seemed to have little trouble hearing me. He has a little trouble walking more than very short distances, but still drives. Dorothy has never driven but Jim used to drive to Vienna to visit the family there. Now they just drive out into the countryside, up towards Scotland on the Jedburgh road to Coldstream.

Jim uses a computer with confidence and answers emails very promptly. Both Jim and Dorothy are dressed in smart rather formal clothes, he in tweedy jacket complete with poppy and small enamel badges, shirt and tie, polished black shoes, she in smart skirt, heeled shoes, knitted jacket with brass buttons, jewellery, and very neatly done hair.

I asked about their name of Tod with one d. It's Scots, as Jim is, an old Scots word and means fox. Jim studied his ancestry back to 1700, it was his project on retirement and the reason he first bought a computer and learned how to use it, back in the sixties! He retired at 64. He now has a new screen and a webcam and uses the internet.

Jim also took up making Northumbrian pipes in his retirement. He learned wood-turning at an evening class to make the pipe parts and did quite a few sets of them which he gave to the Pipers Society to hire out.

They fill their days, Dorothy by housekeeping, gardening and cooking, both do shopping, he drives them there and uses an electric cart inside the supermarket. They keep up with family every day by phone and email. Jim does 'Codebreaker' puzzles every day too. He goes to the Probus Club for retired men each week. Family keep an eye on them and so do neighbours. When there was a power cut, the lady opposite came over to bring them hot drinks as she has a gas hob.

Jim still has a strong Scots accent though living in England for so long. Before they moved here 42 years ago, they lived all over Scotland. Interestingly, Dorothy has a marked Scots accent too. Later on I found out that she's not a Scot. She has picked it up from him, presumably, the only time I've encountered this. She said, 'He's the only person I speak to!' He denied this laughing, saying she speaks to lots of people. Their younger daughter lives and works in Austria and is married to an Austrian. They brought up their children to be bilingual, by him speaking German, and she English, to them at all times in the house, and the children only speaking English with their grandparents in the long holidays. One day years on, they were astonished to catch their father speaking English to Jim, their 'Opa'! The other two children live in the Manchester area and in London.

I asked Jim about his war service, as he was wearing a Veterans' Association pin and also an Arctic Star. He was called up in 1940, at age 20, he volunteered for the RAF. He'd been an apprentice electrician so became an electrician working on aeroplanes. He was posted all over, ending up in Oban in 2-10 Squadron, Coastal Command. Though he was supposed to be ground crew, he ended up flying to the Shetland Isles. He was maintaining the planes which were flying boats. Then in September '42, he flew to Russia, to cover a convoy in a

Catalina flying boat, which could stay in the air for 20 hours, searching for submarines. He was in Russia for 4-5 weeks. He said 'The Russian people were lovely. We were very well treated. They had film showings and dances at the community centres. We'd watch the films, so they got English language films in specially for us – Pinocchio and Huckleberry Finn! The locals liked them too.'

After Russia, Jim was posted to Gibraltar and then to Poole harbour and then to Pembroke Dock with the 2-28 squadron. While in Poole, he met Dorothy his wife. She was working in a munitions factory with her sister. They had 'skittle alleys' in Poole and the factory and the RAF both had teams which played against each other. Dorothy and Jim were watching her sister and his mates play and that's how they met and started courting. Dorothy's mother was a widow who got a house in Poole through Dorothy's sister, if they worked at the factory, though they were from London. After Victory in Europe, the RAF and Navy personnel were transferred to the Army, so Dorothy wanted them to marry at once so Jim would still have his much nicer RAF uniform for the wedding pictures! They married in 1945 so have been married for 65years. They got a card from the Queen for their sixtieth anniversary. Jim worked as an electrical engineer, and moved to the north east of England to work for the hospital board, designing installations for the hospitals. Rake Lane was his last big job. Dorothy had part-time jobs in shops in Scotland, in between bringing up the three children, and when they moved here, one daughter was already away at college. Dorothy got a job at 'the ministry', the DHSS in Newcastle.

I asked them how they feel about their lives now.

Jim: 'Our family keeps tabs on us. Our daughter in Austria phones every day.'

Dorothy: 'They all come, at different times.'

Jim: 'Each child had their own room here which they could decorate as they liked. I was determined they'd have a room each, including the one who'd already left home. Our son comes up for work and stays. They all stay in their own rooms when they come to visit.'

Dorothy: 'We've done nothing special, we've just had a happy family life.'

RAY, 89

Still independent and involved, after a busy productive life and
active war service.

I'll be ninety soon. I live in my own house in a good area. It's got four bedrooms
but I like it! I'm not going anywhere! I've lived here for 45 years. I live
independently, and alone with the dog since my wife died nine years ago. I have
a cleaner coming in two hours a week, and my late wife's nurse who looked after
her in her last illness, still comes round once a week for a chat and helps me
around the house a bit. I have a stepdaughter whom I see once or twice a year. I
keep busy by being on committees, I'm on the Cricket Club committee, and now
Royal Grammar School are connected with it, I liaise with them. I'm in their Old
Boys Association too. I was in the Residents' Association for many years until
fairly recently. I've put in my will, that when I die, my house must be sold to a
family or couple, for the sake of the neighbours, so they don't get multiple
occupancy next door. I get out a lot, I take the dog for walks, I walk at least two
and a half miles each day, and twice a week I walk all the way into town. I do
still drive, up to about thirty mile distances, but I prefer to walk. We used to travel
to Holland a lot, but since we got the dog, not so much. I've not been for 2 or 3
years. But our friends there come to stay here! I'm going next time by ferry,
flying is so uncivilised, all that waiting around being herded about in airports. I
used to do a lot of flying, to the States several times for example. I have no
computer, I have no wish to learn about them, I have a steam radio and a steam
TV! I'm in good health, I have three monthly checkups. I do my own gardening,
except for the heavy digging. I keep my brain going by doing crosswords, I do
two per day, in the local daily paper. I have loads of friends but I do get lonely,
it's coming back to an empty house with nobody to ask how your day's been. I
miss the affection I had from my wife, Robbie.

I was at RGS 1932-7. I met an old school friend at a funeral recently, he was
amazed how well I am. I visited an old friend in a care home, he's got dementia,
he asked me, why have they put me in here and not you?!

My wife Robbie was five years younger than me. She was a professional
freelance model, for Jaeger. She used to do shows up here. I met her in the Eldon

Grill Bar one night in 1958. We married in 1963. She packed in modelling later on and worked for an architect. She had one daughter, who was 11 or 12 then. We didn't have any children. We were married just on 40 years. We used to travel together, and independently. After we got the dog, we'd take turns. I'd go to Holland, then she'd go to Malta.

I used to be in farming and agriculture. I was in the Territorial Army so I got called up for the army just before the war started in 1938. I was in the desert fighting when I was 20. 1941, I was in Italy, and later at D Day. I was in tanks and armoured cars. I was wounded three times, twice in the desert, once in Italy. That didn't affect my health too much but I did have what's now called Post-traumatic Stress Disorder after but I was ok pretty soon. I went over to the US to work after the war but then my brother died, at 31, from polio, then it was the scourge of Newcastle. So I felt I had to come back. I wanted to get into the commercial side of farming. My father had a farm with another man, it was sold because I didn't want to take it on, though I loved lambing, and working with the sheep. So I joined West Cumberland Farmers, selling and buying and marketing grain from them, to mills and so on. I ended up with 26 branches between Perth and Lincoln.

So I keep busy and active, and totally independent. If I feel a bit down, I look in the mirror, and say to myself, come on you silly old bugger, you can still walk, talk, eat, what's the matter with you!

RENDA, 89
Happily married to Cyril, and independent, with a loving family far
and near, uses skype to keep in touch.

Known as 'Renda', as her middle name is Marenda, she is 89. A lovely woman, warm and chatty and with a laugh in her voice, so cheerful and you could tell really motherly but with an independent streak. She lives with her husband Cyril, they just had their 65th wedding anniversary. He's 18 months younger. They met when 16 and 17! 'We are very very lucky and we do appreciate it.' They've lived in their own three bedroomed semi for over 50 years! 'We're not nomads'.

They are very family oriented. Two daughters, four grandchildren, seven great grandchildren, one just born and one on the way. One daughter and her family live in Denmark. Renda and Cyril have been there four times, and Renda once alone. Their daughter comes over four times every year, flies to Edinburgh and trains down, and they all drive up to Craster and rent a house overlooking the sea for three weeks, this has gone on every year for years. That's been and is their main holiday. Their other daughter lives near Hull out in beautiful countryside in a hamlet with big houses, big gardens and big 'neckbreaking' trees. They go down there, they used to drive but now go by rail. 'I love trains, I get excited in the station.'

They live totally independently, she does all her own housework, he does the stairs and he drives so does all the shopping. They have no outside help. 'We do everything as we've always done it.'

They have no computer but when their daughter brings her laptop they skype to New Zealand relatives. Her husband, a keen organist, now plays electric keyboards. They were Chair and Vice Chair, on the committee of the Electronic Organ Society, for many years. When Renda retired at 57 she joined the League of Friends at a nearby hospital, worked there for 20 years and loved it. They first met at age 16 and 17, walking down the road to work at Parsons Chemical Laboratories. They married at 23&24, three weeks after war ended. He was a chartered electrical engineer, he was a designer at Parsons. They worked there through the war, it was a reserved occupation. She gave up work to bring up her daughters and then in her forties worked for Scottish and Newcastle Breweries for 17 years. They see family a lot and Renda knits, especially for all the babies - she loves babies.

One daughter is doing the family tree, Renda finds it's bringing back memories talking about this with her. She remembers at about six or seven years old, watching them build the Tyne Bridge, when she lived in Gateshead. Her Aunt told her they'd have to walk over the arch! She remembers the king and queen coming in an open horse drawn carriage to open the bridge. Queen Mary was stiff, like she had something down her back, not even a smile! Renda was terrified of the bridge as when they walked over it she was told not to walk near the railings as the platform would tip over!

Renda loved doing the 85+ project, as she could tell her interviewer was approving of her and she found she could do everything she was asked, including things she didn't know she could do. A nice doctor came with very expensive heart equipment and explained everything and she was really interested. She enjoyed the special 85+ lunch and met me there, she was last to leave as she was waiting for her husband to collect her in the car.

Renda and Cyril are very happy and love the way their lives are now. They are very family centred, but Renda said they make sure the family knows they make their own decisions about what they do.

CHANGING AGE, CHANGING MINDS
ACKNOWLEDGEMENTS.

Grateful thanks are due to the following people and organisations, for enabling me to meet and interview the participants.

For my Residency, at the Institute for Ageing and Health, University of Newcastle upon Tyne: Professor Tom Kirkwood CBE, Dr Lynne Corner and Graham Armitage for supporting my Residency, and Professor Louise Robinson and Professor Julian Hughes for helping me establish contacts for this book. Funding is by Newcastle University's societal theme, *Changing Age*. IAH staff have helped me with my work, their input to my poetry is acknowledged in *All That Lives,* my collection.

85+: Karen Davies for putting me in touch with volunteers from the project.

Organisations for Older People:

Dementia Care Partnership: in particular, Rani Svanberg, and Kay at Bradbury Centre, Christine and Caroline at Shafto Centre, and Joanne, manager of day centres for liaison.

Age Concern: Sue Pearson, Regional Director, and Julie Home, who organised my visits to AC day centres.

Alzheimer's Society: Carol Metcalfe who organised my visits to their centres.

Marden High School: especially Joan Bloomfield, also Alison Abbott and of course the students from Year Seven and Year Ten who took part in workshops.

Writer Char March for arranging my Residency with Leeds hospitals (through TONIC), also staff and patients of LGI and the Bexley Cancer Wing at Jimmy's.

And of course, thank you to all the participants for sharing their stories.

Valerie Laws